African Merchants
of the Indian Ocean

African Merchants
of the Indian Ocean

Swahili of the
East African Coast

John Middleton
Yale University

WAVELAND
PRESS, INC.
Long Grove, Illinois

For information about this book, contact:
Waveland Press, Inc.
4180 IL Route 83, Suite 101
Long Grove, IL 60047-9580
(847) 634-0081
info@waveland.com
www.waveland.com

Illustrations

Cover: A small dhow in Lamu harbor, northern Kenya, used as a local ferry for passengers between Lamu and the many nearby islands and the mainland from which a road goes south to Mombasa. These ferries sail whenever there are enough passengers. They can sail to more distant ports, even as far as Somalia, southern Arabia, and Madagascar as well as southward along the coast to Mombasa and Zanzibar. A typical crew is the captain and a single sailor. *(Photo by Justine Baruch)*

The illustrations in this book show various places and people on the Swahili coast. Swahili people usually do not like photographs to be taken of themselves as individuals, and are against their publication unless they give permission. I have therefore not shown individual people with the exception of the photograph on page 65, that of a very old friend for whom this book is dedicated.

I am grateful to Yale University Press for permission to reproduce the map of the Swahili coast.

Copyright © 2004 by Waveland Press, Inc.

ISBN 1-57766-314-4

Printed in the United States of America

7 6 5 4 3 2 1

to the memory of

Sheikh Athman Basheikh
of Lamu

CONTENTS

vii

PREFACE

This is a short book on an unusual people of eastern Africa, those known as Swahili. Much of the world knows their name but little about them and their civilization. One reason is that they do not easily fit into the general Western picture of "African" peoples. As international merchants for over more than a thousand years they are different from the kinds of peoples usually studied by anthropologists and historians. In this book I describe and consider their society and civilization to show their importance both for anthropologists and for others interested in Africa. There are many writings about them, some by Swahili scholars, of diverse focus and unequal quality, and I use my own personal knowledge to put all these many bits and pieces of information together to make a coherent account. I have divided the book into chapters arranged to show Swahili civilization both what it is today and what it was in the past. It is a somewhat personal selection of what I see as the principal facts about Swahili. Those Swahili scholars who have read my earlier writings have agreed that what I have done there makes sense for them, and I hope they will think the same of this book. But then Swahili are the most courteous of people.

I should say something of my own qualifications for thinking that I may write about people whom I have known for half a century. Any ethnographic account is a personal one of the writer's experiences of what he or she has seen and heard. It is also a joint one, written in conjunction with the people concerned, without whom the ethnographer can do nothing.

I first visited the country of the Swahili people in 1944, when in the British army I spent almost a year in the city of Mombasa, on the coast of Kenya. In 1958 I was invited to make a study of land use and tenure in the then sultanate of Zanzibar, at a time when there was much political dissension over land rights between local Swahili and immigrant Arabs of the sultanate. In 1986 I spent a year in the northern Swahili town of Lamu, to learn about patterns of family and marriage; I have followed that by shorter visits in later years.

ACKNOWLEDGMENTS

Many people have helped me write this book. Some are thanked in previous books. Here I add the names of those with whom I have discussed this present one: Bwana Athman Lali Omar, Ms. Kana Dower, Dr. Michelle Gilbert, Dr. Helle Goldman, Sheikh Mohamed Hyder, Mr. Bruce McKim, Sheikh Ahmed Sheikh Nabahany, and Dr. Kimani Njogu.

I thank Justine Baruch, who generously spent many hours making this a far better and more readable book than it was when I first showed it to her. I also thank Jeni Ogilvie for her excellent editing and clearing up my more ambiguous passages.

I wish also to thank the governments of Zanzibar and Kenya, the Fulbright-Hays Research Committee, and the Yale University Center for International and Area Studies, for their support and encouragement.

I thank Yale University Press for permission to reproduce the map of the Swahili coast from my *The World of the Swahili*, New Haven, 1992. I also thank Justine Baruch, Michelle Gilbert, Dominique Malaquais, and Nancy Nooter for allowing me to reproduce their photographs.

The excerpt from the poem *Al-Inkishafi* on pages 132–134 is taken from Sayyid Abdalla bin Ali bin Nasir, translated by James de Vere Allen and published in 1977 by the East African Literature Bureau, Nairobi. James Allen held the copyright and before his death kindly gave me permission to reproduce passages from it.

African Merchants
of the Indian Ocean

The Swahili Coast

1

WHY SWAHILI?

This book is about people who are generally known as Swahili. The proper form used in East Africa is the plural, WaSwahili, but the root form is so widely used for them by non-Swahili that I do the same. They live in a string of some two hundred settlements, from small villages to large cities, along the thousand miles of narrow coastline from Somalia to Mozambique and on the offshore islands. They number about three hundred thousand people in the nations of Kenya and Tanzania, with others in the Comoro Islands, Madagascar, Somalia, Mozambique, the Democratic Republic of the Congo, and southern Arabia. They are very diverse in their everyday ways of living, social position, wealth, houses and gardens, and dialects of the KiSwahili language, yet they form a single society with a single civilization.

A visitor, whether trader, government official, sailor, African from another country, or tourist, sees the Swahili coast, the western shore of the Indian Ocean, as one of great natural beauty, with long offshore reefs, lagoons of pale green water, white sand beaches, and a line of scattered towns and villages, mostly of white-walled and thatched houses set among coconut palms. For the last half-century it has been a favored place for tourists, most of whom pay

1

brief visits to the European-owned hotels on the coast, each with its semiprivate beach. They are rarely interested in the human beings who live there; yet it is they, the WaSwahili, "the People of the Coast," who own the towns and the beaches, and whose civilization is many centuries older than many of those of visitors who patronize them as "The Natives."

Swahili Language and Names

The Swahili language, KiSwahili, is a member of the Bantu language family, which covers most of Africa south of the equator. Bantu languages add noun-prefixes to the roots of words. A single Swahili person is Mswahili, while two or more people are referred to as WaSwahili. The language is KiSwahili; the prefix Ki- is also used to refer to the general culture of a people, so that KiSwahili can mean "in the Swahili fashion" (for example, of houses or clothing). In many Bantu languages there is also a prefix U-, to mean "land of," but USwahili is never used, presumably because there is no single bounded Swahili political territory. A suffix -ni, as in Swahilini, is occasionally heard for the northern Swahili coast as the place where WaSwahili emerged as a distinct people, but it is not in common use. In this book I generally use merely the root form Swahili for the people.

Many writers on Swahili try to define a single "Swahili" identity, seen typically in terms of an unchanging "ethnicity," a common language and culture, and adherence to Islam. These attempts fail to appreciate that an "identity" is fluid, ever changing in the conflicts and contradictions of social life and history. It is defined and often invented anew so as to create and validate a sense of belonging to a particular community. In their own view only the "People of the Coast" are properly Swahili. Others who live along and near the coast, such as the Mijikenda, Zaramo, and Digo, are not, although visitors often confuse them. To know who are Swahili and why they are important, we must understand the underlying structure of their society and its history and put both their and our own ideas of ethnicity, culture, history, and ties with other peoples into their proper contexts.

This is not a simple thing to do, and Swahili are not simple people to understand. If we read the accounts of them by different writers, we see what at first sight appears to be confusion and contradiction. They are said to be merchants and yet fishermen, to live in both cities and yet small villages, to reckon various kinds of kinship and marriage, to be Africans and yet Arabs. All these statements are more or less accurate in respect of one or another Swahili group, town, or stretch of coastline, but not for all of them. Some writers assume that this variety is a sign of breakdown or "detribalization," but this is mistaken; it is rather a sign of the ability to adjust to ever-changing circumstances. To clarify and understand them we must perceive Swahili people as living in many distinct local communities that they link together in various ways to form a single civilization.

Swahili people are Africans: they live in Africa, their history and present condition are part of Africa, and their future will continue to be so. Most of them consider themselves to be of Africa, but with differences from other Africans, and with their own unique civilization of which they are deeply proud. In the past they were often considered to have Arabian and Persian origins, a view without historically reliable foundation. Their culture does contain many traits that have come from Arabia, in particular their religion, Islam, which reached the coast in the eighth century with the settlement of a few Arab traders, although it took a century or two to be accepted by the local people. This does not mean that they are a creole people from Asia with an "oriental" culture, as some writers have stated. Their language has many words with

Swahili Poetry

Swahili poetry is a highly prized cultural tradition, and the skill of a poet, man or woman, is greatly honored. This poetry is not a form of translation from Arabic but is indigenous to Swahili. Impromptu spoken poetry competitions are popular, both within a town and between towns. Most Swahili poetry is religious or homiletic, although erotic love poems are famous. Records of Swahili poetry go back several centuries, written in Arabic script. Today poets speak their verse on radio and in magazines, much of it political, written with puns, *double entendres*, and "hidden" meanings. Styles of meter, alliteration, and rhyme are complex, and the use of an early dialect known as KiNgozi, no longer spoken and with a wide vocabulary of ancient words, is still common for serious poems.

Arabic roots, but is an African one. Swahili have long been literate, with a sophisticated literature in both prose and poetry that is rare in Africa. Their language has been written for over a millennium in Arabic script; today people use Roman script for most purposes, and the better educated people know the Arabic form as well. Arabic remains the language of the Koran and other sacred writings.

Today Swahili play little part on the national scene of the two countries of which most of them are members, Kenya and Tanzania; yet in past centuries they were widely known and were to be reckoned with by the traders of Asia, the Red Sea, and the interior of Africa. They were merchants in international trade for many centuries, and in this respect they were different from most African peoples. Most societies of the continent have until recently been fairly small in both territory and in numbers, as well as in the scale of their relations with others in trade, marriage, political power, and religion. Swahili, although not all that many in population, have never been isolated or defined as what used to be called a "tribal" or even "primitive" people. They were for many centuries—and still are—merchants and cultural brokers between the interior of Africa and the countries lying on the northern and eastern shores of the Indian Ocean, and this role of long-distance middlemen led them to form their unusual society and civilization.

Three concepts help create the general Swahili view of their world. One is *ustaarabu*, often translated as "civilization," but a better translation is "long-standing and wise tradition." The word is often mistranslated today as "Arabness," but it comes from a root verb -*staarabu*, "to be long lived and wise." The second is *utamaduni*, "urbanity or belonging to a town." Swahili claim these qualities for themselves and contrast them to a third, *ushenzi*, "barbarism," the quality of ignorance and ill manners that they see in all those outside them. To be wise and urbane means that one has "true" Swahili ancestry, purity, honor, trustworthiness, and courtesy, as well as knowledge of the world that comes only from belief in God.

It is often said that Swahili are sunk in nostalgia for their glorious past and unwilling to take advantage of the modern world that they confront. This is no more than patronizing and wishful thinking by those who make the claim. Swahili themselves see their quiet behavior as the expression of their traditional way of life and good manners. They contrast these to the vulgarity and incompetence of so many modern government officials, businesspeople, and tourists. Outside observers do not always understand what they see before them: they talk of the need to "develop" and "modernize" other people whom they cannot understand and whom in the end they regard as inferior, instead of improving their own sensitivity of observation and analysis. Swahili people are perfectly aware of where they stand in the modern world and of what they want to be in it, but few outsiders take the trouble to listen to them.

Most anthropological studies of African societies and their cultures have been limited to the present. The past is all too often considered by anthropologists as marginal, mainly because evidence of it in written records is so often lacking. For Swahili, who do possess written records of their past, their history is an integral part of their tradition and civilization, and in outline at least is known to all Swahili people. It cannot be ignored.

Visitors see things; they gain impressions, understandings, and misunderstandings of what they observe. Swahili civilization may appear to some non-Swahili as confused and even unstable; to others it may appear as old-fashioned and even quaint, perhaps a sign of stability. Both views are partial and in many ways mistaken. The Swahili past is not only a determinant of the present but very much part of it. Swahili people are fully aware of both the loss of their former supremacy over the coast and also of the opportunities that modernization may give them to regain that supremacy. Their own knowledge of their past gives them a sense of purpose and steadfastness in an uncertain and dangerous present. If we outsiders are to understand Swahili civilization, we must perceive the Swahili view of both present and past. This is what this book is about.

Further Reading

For this introductory chapter, I give some general references. Those marked * have full bibliographies and are especially useful as sources for journal articles that I do not list, as there are so many of them.

*John Middleton. 1992. *The World of the Swahili: An African Mercantile Civilization*. New Haven: Yale University Press (paperback 1997). [A general anthropological account covering most aspects of Swahili civilization.]

*Mark Horton and John Middleton. 2000. *The Swahili: The Social Landscape of a Mercantile Society*. Oxford and Malden: Blackwell. [An account with more emphasis on prehistory and history than the previous one.]

A. M. Mazrui and I. N. Shariff. 1994. *The Swahili*. Trenton: Africa World Press. [A general account with emphasis on language and literature.]

C. M. Kusimba. 1999. *The Rise and Fall of Swahili States*. Walnut Creek, CA: Altamira Press. [An excellent account of Swahili history.]

A. H. J. Prins. 1967. *The Swahili-speaking Peoples of the East African Coast*. London: International African Institute. [A general survey of Swahili society, although now rather outdated.]

Abdul Sheriff. 1987. *Slaves, Ivory, and Spices in Zanzibar*. London: James Currey. [A very full history of eighteenth- and nineteenth-century Zanzibar trade.]

Derek Nurse and Thomas Spear. 1985. *The Swahili: Reconstructing the History and Language of an African Society, 800–1500*. Philadelphia: University of Pennsylvania Press. [The early history of Swahili.]

Michael N. Pearson. 1989. *Port Cities and Intruders: The Swahili Coast, India, and Portugal in the Early Modern Era*. Baltimore: Johns Hopkins University Press. [An excellent account of the wider background to Swahili society.]

Jan Knappert. 1979. *Four Centuries of Swahili Verse*. London: Heinemann. [An anthology of Swahili poetry.]

Frederick Johnson. 1939. *A Standard Swahili-English Dictionary*. London: Oxford University Press. [The best easy-to-use dictionary.]

2

THE SEA AND THE LAND

Swahili people form a society made up of many distinct communities and settlements dispersed along the coastline of eastern Africa and on the adjacent islands; virtually every Swahili settlement is at most only a mile or two away from the ocean. They have lived on this coast since they first became recognizable as a distinct society in the eighth and ninth centuries, and their geographical situation enabled them to act as merchants for more than the next thousand years. They have never been isolated, but always linked to their non-Swahili neighbors and the more distant peoples with whom they traded, and they have been important throughout the history of eastern Africa and the western Indian Ocean.

The Swahili Coast

The East African coast stretches from Cape Guardafui in the far north of Somalia to the coast of South Africa near the modern city of Durban. Not all of it is fertile and a good deal of it is little populated. The rich thousand-mile Swahili coast proper is at its center, from near Mogadishu, the capital of Somalia, to the central part of the coast of Mozambique. A few miles from the coastline

7

itself are the large islands of Zanzibar (known locally as Unguja), Pemba, and Mafia. Farther away to the east are the Comoro islands, whose people are not always considered to be "real" Swahili; due to their colonial history under France, they are linked to Madagascar rather than to the African coast. Other peoples live immediately behind them and in some places are interspersed with them: their economies and histories are closely linked to those of Swahili, but they are never considered to be Swahili.

This thousand-mile stretch of coastline is not uniform. There are marked variations in the patterns of reefs and lagoons, the sizes of the rivers that cross it to empty into the ocean, the many islands and islets, the richness of the soils and the sea, and the uses made of them. The coastal sea- and landscapes are one. Although they limit the range of livelihoods available to Swahili people, they have also largely been formed by their inhabitants and are central features in these inhabitants' histories, myths, and everyday knowledge of the world in which they live. Swahili are very much a maritime people, and most of them live within sight and even sound of the sea. Their traditional means of travel and transport are by sailing vessels that range from great dhows to small canoes. The roads along the coastline are often impassable by floods, and then ship and air remain the only ways to travel.

The coastal climate is mild even though tropical. It can be very hot, especially in the dry season from December to February, but the heat is tempered by sea breezes. The rainfall is good, averaging some thousand millimeters a year, generally becoming less the farther inland from the coastline. It is heaviest in March and April, and there are lesser rains in the late summer. The rains give the more densely cultivated parts of the coastline the appearance of green and fertile gardens, although some areas are too poor to support many crops other than the ubiquitous coconut palm, which can grow in poor and sandy soils. Early travelers from Arabia and Europe saw the coast as a virtual paradise of beauty and abundance.

Richness of the Sea

The environment consists of several parts: the ocean, the reefs, the lagoons, and the beaches; the rivers and creeks; the low-lying coastal plains that form a narrow strip of land behind the beaches; and the higher and hilly land behind that. In the north there is inland an arid semidesert known as the Nyika, and there are dry plains behind most of the southern part of the coast. In some parts of northern Tanzania fertile mountains come down almost to the coastline. Behind all are the savannas, highlands, and great lakes of the interior proper. Each of these regions produces different kinds of foodstuffs; wood; iron and copper; elephant and hippopotamus ivory; hides and skins; and many other things for the long-distance trade from Africa to Asia that went through the Swahili settlements at the coast. The various regions are inhabited by peoples of different economies, political systems, forms of social organization, cultures, and languages. Most of their inhabitants have at one time or other been in direct or indirect contact with the Swahili merchants in the coastal settlements.

The Indian Ocean, unlike the Atlantic or the Pacific, is small enough to permit a close network of sailing routes between the lands that surround it. All of them are linked by their reliance on each other—each producing things (metals, animal products, spices, slaves, and other commodities) needed by the others. Sailing between them is based on the regular and predictable monsoons between India and Africa. The northeast monsoon blows from November until March, being strongest during December and January; it brings the dhows from Asia to eastern Africa. The southwest monsoon blows from June until October, and is at its height during August and September; it takes ships from Africa to Asia. Between the monsoons the winds are uncertain and unreliable, and sailing beyond the immediate coast can be dangerous for small vessels. The times vary slightly from one year to another, but the pattern is reliable enough for sailors—Arab, Swahili, Indian, and even Chinese—to plan and to make long journeys across the ocean. Dhows still sail from the Swahili ports to Arabia and India and back, a journey that may take some two months. Without the monsoons Swahili society could never have come into existence: instead of mercantile ports there would have been merely a series of fishing villages.

The ocean is more than an economic resource to Swahili people. The sea, *bahari,* is the place from which comes potential wealth in the form of sailors and traders who bring goods such as cloth, beads, porcelain, arms, exotic furniture and foods, fashions in clothing and ornament, and modern things such as films and videos. It brought Islam and writing, as well as colonial conquerors and Turkish, Egyptian, and European pirates. The ocean is a place of immense power and danger, the home of many spirits (see chapter 13); yet it may be tamed and used by those living on its shores

Swahili Sailing Ships

There are many kinds of Swahili sailing ships. The earliest, no longer made but still remembered along the coast, was the *mtepe*, a vessel with the hull made of planks tied together by rope, without nails, and caulked with fish oil. The largest ocean-going vessel, which Western writers call dhow, is properly *jahazi*. The *dau* is a small sailing boat for local use. There are also the double-outrigger canoes, originally brought from Indonesia by early immigrants, and smaller canoes and fishing vessels of many kinds. The great jahazi, still built in a few places on the Swahili coast that are famed for ship-building and repair, can sail as far as Arabia and India.

Today all these vessels have modern canvas sails, but in the past the smaller ones had sails of coconut palm leaf. Swahili seafarers have known of the compass for centuries, although most rely on their own detailed knowledge of the coast and ocean. Almost all Swahili ships are painted near the bow with *oculi*, "eyes" that protect them from evil spirits.

Sailing races are a favorite sport and sailors take immense care to keep their faster craft in good condition for it.

if, as Swahili say, they listen to the words of God who created it. A famous Swahili scholar in Mombasa told me that poets gain knowledge and skill by "going to the bottom of the sea, where they find many secrets."

Much of the coastline is bounded by long coral reefs that break the force of the Indian Ocean. The reefs have gaps where rivers discharge, because fresh water discourages the growth of coral. The larger Swahili settlements are ports behind or near these openings, so that sailing vessels can reach them. They are usually sited on the leeward side of small islands or at the heads of creeks and rivers, providing safe anchorage and protection from both the sea and from human marauders inland. They are in places with reliable water supplies, the sweet water lying above the heavier salt seawater, so that wells on which the settlements depend can be shallow.

Inside the reefs are shallow and calm lagoons that support fish and shellfish, and in many of them are forests of mangrove trees used for building timber. Today port industries, agricultural development, overfishing, severe mangrove cutting, and tourist industries are destroying the reef system on which the coastal region depends. The fragile environment has supported the Swahili settlements for many centuries; today it is in great danger from modern development and its viable future is uncertain.

Towns along the Shore

The coast has several large modern towns and cities, the most important being Mombasa, Dar es Salaam, Zanzibar City, and Tanga. Like all modern cities they have cosmopolitan populations. There are many ancient Swahili towns of narrow streets and stone-built houses, such as Pate, Lamu, Malindi, Pangani, Bagamoyo, and others, all today inhabited by Swahili and some by non-Swahili immigrants as well. Interspersed with the towns are villages, which are large rural clusters of houses and gardens. Many places are mainly ruins from the great glories of the past; settlements are built literally among them, as at Kilwa or Pate. Other places, such as Gedi behind Malindi, have ancient and elaborate stone buildings that are now deserted and filled with bats and ghosts.

The large offshore islands of Zanzibar and Pemba are rather apart. Zanzibar's history has been separate from the rest of the coast: it was for over two centuries the capital of an immigrant Arab sultanate, which exercised colonial overrule over the Swahili. Pemba island, known in Arabic as al-Khudra, "the green one," is perhaps the most fertile part of the entire coast. For centuries it has provided rice, the preferred staple, and other foodstuffs to the coastal towns, and its plantations and farms are the principal source of the cloves that have long been the main export crop of Zanzibar. The two islands today form a province of the Republic of Tanzania.

A few long rivers pass through the coastal region to empty into the Indian Ocean: from north to south the Juba, Tana, Sabaki, Pangani, Rufiji, and Rovuma. All support riverine populations growing some specialized crops, especially rice and fish. None are easily navigable far inland due to rapids, shoals, and shallow water. There are traces of former rivers, now dried up, in the far north, which were probably early routes for trade with southern Ethiopia.

The mainland behind the narrow Swahili coastline includes mostly hilly country inhabited by non-Swahili farmers; there are also several stretches of arid semidesert occupied by pastoralists, hunters, and foragers. All these groups have long been linked to the Swahili towns as suppliers of trade goods such as ivory, hides and skins, copal, incense and other resins. Some of them, especially pastoralists such as Maasai and Oromo, have often been raiders on the wealthy coastal settlements. Today the raiders include refugees from Somalia, armed with modern rifles, who have driven Swahili from many of their northern settlements and have made farming, hunting, and travel on the northern mainland dangerous and often impossible.

Behind the coastal lands is the higher and generally fertile interior. This immense region is linked to the coast by only fragile communications, formerly by foot caravans and today by unreliable roads and railways. For centuries its peoples supplied Swahili with trade goods, mainly ivory, slaves, gold, rock crystal, and copper. In return they received manufactured commodities from Asia, mainly cloth, beads, and luxury goods. Today the interior supplies the coast with unskilled laborers, who replace the former slaves, a development that has greatly changed the composition of the coastal population.

Marine Economy

The lagoons, the beaches, and the reefs together provide the marine resources that Swahili use for much of their food and other needs. Both the land and the lagoons within the reefs are divided

Small sailing dhows in the harbor of Mkokotoni, in northern Zanzibar island and once a port used for carrying slaves to Arabia. They sail throughout the day to and from the nearby small island of Tumbatu, the dark line visible in the distance. Tumbatu has three villages but little water or fertile soil: the dhows carry local farmers from Tumbatu to farm near Mkokotoni and also take cans and jars of water to the island. *(Photo by author)*

into productive areas that are owned by descent groups and families, subject to Islamic law and inheritance, and carefully protected against the anger of the spirits that are thought to dwell in them.

A valuable resource is that of mangrove forests that grow in the saltwater swamps and provide wood used to build houses. The wood is hard, heavy (it does not float), long-lasting, and immune to termites. It is also used for charcoal, tannin, and several local medicines. Mangrove trees spread quickly and block rivers and harbors if not continually harvested: many once-important ports are today almost unusable by the silting brought about by mangrove forests, as they prevent the free movement of tidewater. Mangrove cutting is physically hard and dangerous work (venomous snakes live among the trees), formerly done by slaves and today done by only the poorest laborers. The trees also provide shelter for fish and shellfish, the former being the main food along the coastline (shellfish are forbidden as food under Islamic law, but are sold to the tourist hotels along the coast). The actual reefs are also rich in marine life and provide the coral for building the "stone" houses of the larger towns. Today the beaches, lagoons, and reefs form the main attractions for visiting tourists. The large number of tourists and their activities and needs are leading to serious degradation of these areas, from the destruction of the coral reefs by scuba diving to salination of wells due to taking in too much fresh water so that the underlying salt water rises up into them.

Swahili Gardens

The Swahili coast is in places very fertile, especially the islands of Zanzibar and Pemba, and produces an immense range of foodstuffs. For vegetables, people grow several kinds of sorghums and millets, cassava, sesame, many varieties of peas and beans, eggplant, sweet potato, taro (cocoyam), tomatoes, basil, tamarind, and chili peppers. For fruit they plant bananas, oranges and other citrus, mangoes, jackfruit, breadfruit, lychees, and jujube. They grow kapok for bedding, ylang-ylang for fragrance, and tobacco. They plant many kinds of palms: the valuable and ubiquitous coconut (which produces coconut milk, oil, copra, fibers, and wood), areca (used with betel nut for chewing), raffia, and many others. And they grow bourbon roses, jasmine, and flowers used in women's corsages and to scatter on the ground at the *ntazanyao* ceremony that concludes a wedding.

The narrow strip behind the beaches is the site of Swahili settlements and their fertilized gardens and fields, which often give two food crops a year. In earlier centuries the Swahili grew indigenous cotton that was the base for a famed weaving industry: in the sixteenth century Portuguese travelers wrote that Swahili weaving was the finest in the world.

Near the coast also in the nineteenth and twentieth centuries Arab, Indian, and European landowners and companies opened large plantations to grow grains, cloves, sisal, sugarcane, and rubber. Today only those for sisal and cloves are still in production, labor shortage being endemic since the abolition of slavery at the turn of the twentieth century.

Social Geography of the Coast

The long coast is not uniform. Each stretch is distinct in climate, inhabitants, ethnic identities and occupations, means of production and distribution, histories, and patterns of settlement and building. Swahili people see their coast as a set of discrete yet interlinked settlements and named stretches of coastline, each with its own history, economy, and links with the others. Swahili ocean fishermen and dhow captains sail all along the coast and know every port, reef, river mouth, and dangerous tide.

The coast of Somalia, in the far north, was a few centuries ago inhabited by Swahili people; until only a few years ago KiSwahili was spoken in Mogadishu and the other coastal towns along what is known as the Benadir coast (Coast of the Harbors) and is generally said to be "lost" land.

Swahili country of today begins in Kenya. Its northern part is known as Pwani ya Visiwani (Coast of Islands). Its islands and creeks contain the ancient towns of the Lamu archipelago, including the present-day Pate, Siyu, Faza, and Lamu, all founded many centuries ago. There are the ruined sites of Shanga, Manda, Ungwana, and other prehistoric Swahili trading ports. This is also the area of the mythical Swahili homeland known as Shungwaya and of the Swahili culture hero Fumo Liongo, whose verses and songs are believed to be among the oldest and most famous Swahili poetry.

Southward lies the Nyali coast, containing the old town of Malindi with its modern hotels and casinos, and the international port and railway terminus of Mombasa, known in KiSwahili as Mvita (Place of War). This stretch of coast was the heartland of

Swahili civilization between the twelfth and the early nineteenth centuries, its larger towns ruled by kings and queens.

South again is the Mrima coast, in modern Tanzania. It includes the cities of Dar es Salaam and Tanga, both large ports and termini of railways to the interior, and also former slaving ports such as Pangani and Bagamoyo, "The Burden of the Heart." Offshore are the islands of Zanzibar, Pemba, and Mafia. South again lies the little-inhabited Ngao coast, with the ruins of the once-great Swahili city of Kilwa. Finally is the Kerimba coast of Mozambique, where Swahili presence faded after its conquest in the sixteenth century by the Portuguese, who held Mozambique as a colony until the late twentieth century.

Swahili people see these stretches of coast in relation to their own hometowns and to the distances and times involved in sailing to them and back. Swahili shipowners and sailors visit them to obtain particular things there or to take their own for exchange. Swahili ships have long sailed—and still sail—along the coast from southern Arabia in the north to Mozambique in the south, to Madagascar to the east, and farther afield to India. Each part has its particular resources: mangrove poles from the Rufiji delta and the Lamu archipelago; grains from Pemba and the Malindi region; salt from the Benadir coast; palm leaves (for roofs) from Zanzibar; cowry shells from the Pwani ya Visiwani to India (for making porcelain and also at one time shipped to western Africa as local money); ivory and slaves from the ports that stood at the ends of caravan routes from the interior; gold through the Ngao and Kerimba ports. An experienced Swahili sailor knows the geography of the entire coast, the goods to be obtained there, and the complicated sailing routes along it and across the western Indian Ocean.

Swahili people also see these stretches of coastline as places where a family may once have come from, or where there may be kin related by ancestry or marriage, or where a famous poet or saint may have lived. Swahili continually visit their kin up and down the coast to attend weddings, funeral rites, and anniversaries, and dhows and ferries sail between the stretches of coast and their islands. Swahili are very conscious of former movements of people along the coast, and collective memory, sailing, and visiting provide a cement that links them all into a single maritime society. However, the links never led to the establishment of a single political state over the entire coast. Mercantile competition between towns prevented it, and there has never even been agreement on a single Islamic center for the whole region except for a vague memory of a mythical Shungwaya homeland, perhaps somewhere in Manda Bay.

The directions north and south along the coast have other meanings. The north is the direction of Mecca and the heart of Islam; it is also the direction of the original ports where Swahili merchants claim to have come from, in distinction to their former slaves who came from the interior to the south and the west, regions of darkness as contrasted to the light of Islam.

The coastal soil fertility, rainfall, and ease of travel and transport by sea limit what the inhabitants can do. However, in general it is the inhabitants themselves who make the coast what it is and who could easily destroy it—as so many new non-Swahili immigrants, who come merely to make quick money, are doing. This is the era of the "global" companies intent on profitable despoliation to an extent beyond which the coast can bear, perhaps to the ruin of the Swahili and other peoples who have used it for centuries, but who also care for and protect it.

Further Reading

The books listed at the end of chapter one contain much general and detailed material on the Swahili coast. More specific to this chapter are:

A. H. J. Prins. 1965. *Sailing from Lamu: A Study of Maritime Culture in Islamic East Africa*. Assen, Netherlands: Van Gorcum. [A classic account of one Swahili town, with detailed descriptions of ships and methods of sailing.]

There are many books on the sailing ships of the Indian Ocean. The most general is:

A. Villiers. 1940. *Sons of Sindbad*. New York: Scribners. [A fine book by a writer with long personal experience of sailing across the Indian Ocean.]

3

THE SHAPE OF SWAHILI SOCIETY

As mentioned previously, Swahili people live in a thin band of settlements along a thousand miles of coastline and islands. Each settlement is distinct in appearance, size, production, composition, and sense of identity. Although the settlements are interdependent in many ways and most are linked by kinship and marriage, the people who live in any one settlement like to see themselves as autonomous. So can we talk of a single "Swahili society" or "Swahili civilization"?

A Society or a Cluster of People?

Visitors to the East African coastal towns almost always consider the people who live in them to be similar to one another, members of a single culture, speaking a single language, wearing the same kinds of clothing, and having a more or less similar life. This is a misunderstanding. If we look more closely we see that Swahili are people with many internal differences of social organization, economy, religious practice, and everyday living. They certainly cannot be considered a "tribe" in the old-fashioned colonial sense. So I use the general word "society." Some writers have pre-

17

ferred the term "Swahili-speaking peoples," as denoting a cluster of people who share a common language. The difficulty is that the language, which has many marked dialects, is used as a *lingua franca* by several million people in eastern and central Africa, and so the term is of little use to define only those living along the coast.

The territory that Swahili people occupy as their "land," *nchi*, is not a clearly bounded area on the ground, but merely a line of settlements, farms, and plantations along the coastline. Most of the people are fishermen and gardeners. An elite minority has been and remain merchants, who in the past were closely linked to another occupational category, the slaves whom they owned and in whom they traded. Swahili people live in towns, yet they are very different from the members of modern urban communities found elsewhere in Africa. Swahili towns have been linked by trade to economies in Asia and elsewhere in Africa; so, as merchants, they have been aware not only of their close neighbors but also of distant trading partners in both Asia and the interior of Africa. Their role as international merchants has long given them a "global" knowledge of the wider world.

Swahili people have also maintained unity by their religion, in their eyes the most important aspect of life. They have been Sunni Muslims, of the mainstream Shafe'i school, since the eighth century. Their rulers of the eighteenth and nineteenth centuries, the Arab sultans of Zanzibar, were of the narrower Ibadhi branch, of Oman, but tolerant in appointing both Ibadhi and Shafe'i judges and teachers. Literacy is universal; the skill of a poet is very highly regarded and is open to and practiced by women. Swahili see their society as a center of piety, scholarship, and civilized and urbane behavior, an *umma* or Islamic community set within a waste of non-Muslim barbarism.

Identity and Ethnicity

Swahili and non-Swahili have long argued whether Swahili are "African" or "Asian." These clumsy geographical terms may denote actual or assumed places of origin, but they refer also to occupation, pattern of settlement, and moral qualities. They are set in the historical context of Swahili as middlemen in the African-Asian trading system, in which, facing both ways, they have played the crucial role of cultural brokers and have stressed their links to both Africa and Asia.

Swahili share the single identity of being "WaSwahili," but at the same time they are divided into several constituent identities, almost always defined in terms of ethnicity. People see themselves as members of several distinct ethnic groups, by using words such as *kabila* (usually translated as tribe), *mji* (town), *asili* (origin), or *taifa* (ethnic group or nation), terms that essentially refer to distinct geographical places of origin. "Origin" here is meant explicitly to denote a place from which a group's ancestors are claimed to have come to their present homes. A few of their ancestors did actually come from Arabia, but the great majority were from the coast itself. We need not talk here about "race." Most people of America and Europe are misled by this superficial notion, a term from biology that is misused in everyday speech to denote a claimed link between skin color and cultural behavior. This is irrelevant to Swahili, who count color of skin as of little importance.

Geographical origins for Swahili denote particular ethnic identities. However, it is not really the geographical places that matter, and in any case virtually all have little or no historical foundation. What is important is that each is linked to a position in the Swahili system of stratification and occupation. This is in no way an egalitarian society, and differences of rank and livelihood are held to be important and to be the consequences of origin. Status and occupation are never fixed but may be changed: an obvious case is that of descendants of slaves who today may claim Swahili or even Arab ancestry, despite having come from the African interior. A particular ethnicity is situational rather than heritable.

"Indigenous" Peoples

Most non-Swahili writers of the nineteenth and twentieth centuries divided Swahili people into indigenous and immigrant groups, even though they together form a single society. It is a convenient way of describing them, but the distinction is basically an occupational one: those who acted as international merchants claim to come from Asia; others, the majority who were never merchants, are said to be indigenous to Africa. In brief, occupation defines "ethnicity."

Almost all Swahili people, other than those of slave ancestry— today not always visible as a distinct category—are considered to be indigenous to the coast. The most numerous are the non-Arab fishermen and farmers of the islands of Zanzibar and Pemba. The former are known as the WaHadimu and the WaTumbatu, and the latter simply as WaPemba. The name Hadimu was usually translated by their Arab rulers as "serfs" or even slaves, indicating Arab superiority as conquerors over the indigenous people of the island. The name is more likely to mean "tributaries," those who pay tribute, as their king in the eighteenth century agreed to pay tribute to the Zanzibar sultans to keep his people free. The other two names are simply geographical: those of the small island of Tumbatu, off the northwest coast of Zanzibar island, and the other of the wealthy island of Pemba, once comprising several small independent kingdoms but in recent times comprising a population of independent fishermen, farmers, and clove growers, few of whom kept slaves. In recent years these three groups have frequently called themselves WaShirazi, "People of Shiraz," that is, of Persia; they thereby distinguish themselves as the pre-Arab inhabitants of the islands and of equal or even older Islamic adherence to the immigrant Arabs of the sultanate. Whether in fact any of the groups are really "indigenous" to the islands is uncertain. They probably came over from the mainland, only some twenty-five miles away, and the claim to Persian origin is extremely doubtful. Their use of these names shows their determination to be considered independent occupants of the islands with their own histories and rights to land.

Somewhat similar are the people known as Bajun, originally fishing people from the northern islands between Kismayu and the Lamu Archipelago, but today driven from their islands by Somali raiders and dispersed along the coast at least as far as the Kenya-Tanzania border. Although looked down on by the more patrician Swahili, they are among the oldest-settled Swahili of all and have been Muslims as far back as has any Swahili group. Another long-standing Swahili group, although few live on the African coast itself, are those of the Comoro Islands, who have little contact with the mainland.

The groups just mentioned are fishermen, farmers, mangrove cutters, sailors, artisans, and laborers of many kinds, living mostly in rural settlements. Other elements of the population were directly involved in long-distance commerce and so less dependent on the local productive economy. Those who may also be classed as "indigenous," in the sense of coming from Africa, are the patricians, their slaves, and descendants of slaves.

Those who are usually considered to be culturally the most "real" Swahili are the merchant elite, a minority despite their historical wealth and importance. They are classed together as *wenyeji*, "owners," or as *waungwana*. The last word might be translated into English by the word "gentry," except that that term has implications of being landowners, which would be inappropriate here, and so "patricians" is better. A closer English term would be "gentlemen," but this is untranslatable and in any case omits women. The waungwana live mainly in the northern towns of the Kenya coast, but their having the quality of *uungwana*, "gentle" and courteous behavior, gives them the status of a cultural elite recognized as such throughout the coast. They claim many ties of descent with clans in southeastern Arabia. A few of these claims may be historically accurate, but most are not.

The patricians both kept and traded slaves, as did also some Bajun, until the abolition of slavery and the slave trade, in 1897 in Tanganyika (as it then was) and Zanzibar, and in 1907 in Kenya. Slaves came from many parts of the interior: until about the twelfth century probably most came from Ethiopia in the north, and later mainly from the more distant interior, the region of Lakes Tanganyika and Nyasa (Malawi). Their descendants are known as *wazalia*, a term meaning "country-born" or "born to the household," born to domestic slaves of patrician households. They are merged into the general "Swahili" population mainly by their movement to the larger towns where their origins can be overlooked.

Immigrants

Other inhabitants of coastal society may be considered as immigrants, some coming to the coast many centuries ago. Immigrants form a minority in total numbers but play important economic, political, and religious roles. The largest immigrant element is of people from Arabia, who became of great importance in Africa due to the influence of Islam, the geographical propinquity of southern Arabia, and the rise and fall of the Arab sultanate of Zanzibar.

The earliest were Hadrami traders from Yemen and that part of it known as Hadramaut. From between the first and about the eleventh centuries they established trading posts down the African coast and became part of the general Swahili population. A small colonial-type trading post, without political control over local peoples, needed only a handful of immigrant traders actually living in it to be effective. Some settled, took local wives, and left descendants; others seem merely to have made seasonal visits. There was a larger immigration of Hadrami between the twelfth and fifteenth centuries: these are often known by writers as the "Old Arabs" who, although in time were accepted as "Swahili," still claim their original membership of clans in Arabia. They include several groups of MaSharifu, descendants of the Prophet, who play distinct religious and legal roles in Swahili towns and are given respect for their assumed piety and power to give blessing, *baraka*.

The second category comprises the Omani Arabs, known locally as Manga, most of whom emigrated from Arabia between the mid-eighteenth and the twentieth centuries as members of the newly established sultanate of Zanzibar. At first the Omani Arabs tried to retain their superior political and social position and despised the Swahili as inferior and conquered people; in time, however, they came to adopt the Swahili language and parts of its culture. Many became almost indistinguishable from the "real" Swahili, even though they emphasized their own genealogical descent from Arabia. The rulers of the sultanate introduced greater Arabic elements in both language and everyday life and set in motion most of the later claims of many higher ranking Swahili families to "good" Arabic ancestry.

A third category consists of other Hadrami Arabs from the Hadramaut and Yemen of southwestern Arabia, who immigrated during the late nineteenth and twentieth centuries and are usually known as WaShihiri (from the Arabian port of es-Shihr from which they sailed). They flourished as retailers and some became wealthy; others became successful religious reformers and innovators. Finally, until the Zanzibar revolution of 1964 there were many poor and low-ranking Omani Arab immigrants who worked as ill-paid urban laborers, servants, and coffee-sellers. They suffered the most during the revolution as they could not afford to buy passage out of Zanzibar, and few of them remain today.

Other immigrants came from the Indian subcontinent at various times from the sixteenth to the twentieth century. Some, especially the Bohora Indians, who are themselves Muslims, have often married into Swahili families. The Indian groups brought with them many fashionable objects of clothing, furniture, and cuisine that are today important parts of Swahili life. They also built their own mosques in the larger towns and introduced modern banking systems to the Swahili coast.

During the later years of the twentieth century, in some of the northern towns the name "Swahili" was used for descendants of slaves. The patricians often called themselves "Arabs" since they claimed Arabian origins, and also came to call themselves waung-wana, a situational or behavioral name or title. Yet both are included as "Swahili," and some writers add to the confusion by calling them "Afro-Arabs," ignoring local distinctions. "Arab" is used to refer to the families whose fathers, grandfathers, and earlier forebears have in recent centuries immigrated from either the Hadramaut or Oman.

These and other "ethnic" names form a series known to all Swahili people but are used in various ways to differentiate social and historical situations where differences in occupation, rank, religious knowledge, wealth, political power, and cultural behavior need to be expressed in words. The patricians, for example, virtually always consider themselves to be a single unit in the wider society, even though membership of that category is often in doubt. There are situations in which some patricians find it useful to distinguish themselves from others, and then they bring into play detailed ethnic distinctions such as particular areas of Arabia or the wider Islamic world from which they claim their ancestors came. Descendants of slaves may divide themselves into those descended from slaves of Zanzibar Arabs or from those of northern Swahili families. The various "ethnic" identities are never totally fixed, and people use them for themselves and others in whatever ways they find most useful in particular situations.

The Place of Zanzibar

Virtually all published accounts of the Swahili coast are concerned with the historical, social, and cultural place of Zanzibar and its former Arab sultanate. For most historians, including Arab scholars, the history of the East African coast is essentially seen as the establishment of the sultanate by immigrant Omani Arabs of southeastern Arabia in the eighteenth and nineteenth centuries, the consequent loss of Swahili autonomy, and the colonization of East Africa by the British. Arabs and Swahili have mingled for more than two centuries, yet Swahili people consider themselves to be distinct. Most East African Arabs speak the KiSwahili language in their homes, and so some historians write of the "Swahili-speaking peoples" to include both categories. However, the situation looks very different when viewed from Zanzibar, from the northern towns, from Dar es Salaam, or from Mombasa. For those who consider themselves to be "real" or "pure" Swahili and not of Arab ancestry, the distinction is patent: they hold it to be culturally and legally valid, running through everyday relationships and making sense of the complex social and cultural compositions of the towns and communities along the coast.

Swahili and Zanzibar Arabs have a long history of dissension, beginning with the conquest of Swahili towns and the virtual destruction of their mercantile economy by the sultanate, and ending with the killing and expulsion of most Arabs in the revolution of 1964. The Arabs who live in Zanzibar City, for example, occupy the wealthy and elegant half of it known as Stone Town; most Swahili live in the poorer section known as Ng'ambo, "The Other Side." It is often difficult to distinguish members of either category by their clothing, and Swahili people recall their ancestors often adopting Arab clothing (such as the *buibui*, the Muslim women's veiled gown) and house furnishings so as to ingratiate themselves with their colonizers. However, especially in Mombasa and other industrialized towns, Swahili and Arabs today see themselves as closely linked in opposition to recent immigrants from the interior. The coastal population may be divided by historical origins, occupations, wealth, and religious schools, but they are linked by this modern opposition. They are divided more by rank and class than by any essentialist ethnicity.

The Wider Coastal World

Not only Swahili and Arabs live on this coast; others have lived there for centuries in a close relationship with Swahili people. Some are ethnically and linguistically closely related but they are always distinguishable from one another. Among them are the mainly non-Muslim peoples known as Mijikenda, in Kenya; further south, in Tanzania, are the Muslim Zaramo, Zigua, Doe, Yao, and other groups. These rural farming groups have lived just behind the coast for many centuries, acting as buffers between the Swahili towns and the predatory pastoralist peoples living behind them—Maasai, Oromo, and others in the north, and farther south the many non-Swahili groups of central Tanzania. The use of these ethnic or "tribal" names must not be taken to mean that they are always clearly defined or that there are marked territorial boundaries between them and Swahili settlements. Mijikenda farmers and coconut growers who become wealthy often claim to be Swahili and build Swahili-like houses, wear Swahili clothes, and attend mosques. By this they escape local familial obligations, can attend Swahili law courts instead of local district ones, and gain greater prestige by being "urbane" and no longer "tribal." But Swahili never accept them as being full Swahili, and they remain "strangers" (*wageni*).

Today there are also many recent refugees from the wars in Somalia, some wealthy (and resented by Swahili whose houses are sold to them by local administrators and entrepreneurs), others desperately poor and without employment. In recent years people from the interior—mainly Gikuyu, Luo, and Nyamwezi—have moved to the coast to find land and work. They are disliked and distrusted as land-grabbers by Swahili. The central governments of the modern states of Kenya and Tanzania—especially Kenya—favor them as "politically reliable" settlers among the more doubtful Muslims, but they are never accepted by the Swahili as other than temporary and unpopular visitors.

Further Reading

The books listed at the end of chapter 1 refer in greater or less detail to the problems of Swahili identity and ethnicity. See also:

James de V. Allen. 1993. *Swahili Origins: Swahili Culture and the Shungwaya Phenomenon.* London: James Currey. [An interesting attempt to make sense of the many puzzles of the origins of the present-day Swahili. Shungwaya is the name of the mythical homeland of the people, somewhere in the area of modern Lamu, although no actual site has yet been found.]

4

MYTH AND HISTORY

Most writers on Africa have called African societies "traditional." This does not mean that they are old-fashioned or refuse to become "modern." It means that people assume, or hope, perhaps even fear, that their children's futures will be the same or very like their own present lives and those of their parents' and grandparents'. All societies have histories, some old and long and others new and short. Most societies see the past as more or less unchanging, and do not always see change as necessarily good in itself but often as some kind of aberration that they cannot control. Swahili know that their society is always changing, but they like to control it themselves rather than have others do it.

The Swahili today are neither "traditional" nor without knowledge of what has happened to them in the past. Their culture is literate, in KiSwahili, Arabic, and English. Their sacred books are written in Arabic, and they have a long tradition of poetry and written chronicles in KiSwahili. They are aware of historical changes and of the meanings of past events that materially and morally affected them as a mercantile society. Furthermore, being merchants in trade between Asia and Africa for centuries, they are well aware of an outside world inhabited by people of different cultures, religions, languages, and histories.

27

The people know of and continually discuss their history, of which they are deeply proud. The coast on which they live is filled with ruins built by their own ancestors; most of their towns are ancient places, so that these memorials of past events are part of their everyday lives. During the twentieth century their economy and place in the political world declined so that their memory of and nostalgia for a glorious past—whether factual or mythical—has come to be increasingly important to them.

While Swahili are literate and have been so for a very long time, modern "Western" historiography is in many respects alien to the way in which they regard their own past. They perceive it largely in terms of myth and genealogy, both linked intimately to the landscape and seascape in which they live. Their myths are in the form of written "chronicles" and poems of many kinds. These often involve the names of actual people, and so are taken to be historically accurate, but the mythopoeic idioms used show that they are nonetheless mythological. Indeed, many of the histories of the Swahili coast written by non-Swahili travelers are in fact little more than myth, even if they are attempts to write "objective" accounts of events and persons. Today there are excellent archaeological records, although their interpretations are subject to much argument. When these records, Swahili myths, and travelers' accounts are put together we can perceive a coherent history of the people and the coast and understand the more important parts of the past as they are seen by the people themselves. These "internal" views are crucial for the understanding of this society and how it functions; they provide a mainspring for Swahili political and social behavior and their reactions to outside events. An old Swahili friend in Lamu said to me, "A man is like the captain of a dhow: he knows where he is, where he comes from, and where he intends to go. On his route he meets storms and pirates, and he makes detours; yet in the end he has made a straight line, thanks be to God."

Swahili Beginnings

The first written record of the people of the East African coast is the *Periplus of the Erychthraean Sea*, a mariners' manual written in Greek in Alexandria, probably in the first century A.D. The *Periplus* describes trade down the Red Sea and into the Indian Ocean. It is not a mythical fancy but a hardheaded account for Egyptian and Greek sailors and traders. It lists the ports along the coast from

Egypt as far south as what we now call the Tana River, with details of trade commodities in demand and available in return. The last place to the south was called Rhapta, the only "emporium" or permanent settlement, and beyond it the coast was thought to curve round to the west to link up with the Atlantic. There has been much argument about the position of Rhapta, but it probably lay between the Tana and Juba rivers among the cluster of early settlements on the mainland opposite from the present-day Lamu Archipelago, the region of the mythical Swahili homeland of Shungwaya. Nothing is said in the *Periplus* about the local people except that they had their own languages and that they exchanged animal skins, ivory, tortoiseshell, rhinoceros horn, and incense in return for cloth, beads, metal wire, iron tools, weapons, glass, and wine. Already the pattern of the trade from then to today is clear: natural and unprocessed commodities from Africa were traded for manufactured or processed ones from elsewhere—the history of exploitative colonial trade throughout the world.

The people mentioned in the *Periplus* and in later Chinese accounts of voyages to eastern Africa (where they captured a giraffe for the emperor), were not Swahili. They were probably Cushitic-speaking hunters, gatherers, and pastoralists, who still live today in southeast Ethiopia and Somalia. They were driven out during the first half of the first millennium by Bantu-speaking farmers. Although we do not know what names they used for themselves, we may assume that they were the direct ancestors of present-day Swahili.

Local modes of production and exchange, religious belief and practice, and forms of marriage seem to have changed very little over the centuries. Cultural ties and practices are remarkably strong and long lasting: things such as clan names can have very long lives, and traces of earlier and similar names are found throughout the present-day coastal population. There has always been continual movement of families up and down the coast, yet the underlying societal structure is astonishingly persistent, as can be seen from recent archaeological research that has excavated ruined settlements of which the presently inhabited towns are virtual replicas.

Growth of Swahili Society

Outside writers, especially those of the older generations of historians and prehistorians, have usually maintained that Swahili, although living in Africa, are not really "Africans" at all. They have been called by such terms as "Afro-Arabs," and their civilization said to be a creole one of Arab culture imported to eastern Africa. This view can no longer be held in the light of recent archaeological and ethnographic research, even though it is still accepted by many Swahili themselves, who wish to distance themselves from both their former African slaves and the present African rulers of independent Kenya and Tanzania. Historically, there have been more immigrants from Arabia than from anywhere else, but not overwhelmingly so. What matters is the use of Arabia as a point of reference for claimed ethnic ancestry and as the home of Islam.

By the eighth century traders very like modern Swahili certainly lived in settlements along the coast. They adopted Islam and thereby became "real" Swahili. Evidence for this early history is in both archaeological and written records. The ruins are of stone buildings and the items first collected by archaeologists were mainly of Chinese porcelain, so they held that these settlements had been founded by immigrants from Asia, mixing with local Africans and becoming an Asian creole society. Recent work has provided a different history, the emphasis changing from that on palaces and imported art objects to locally made houses, pottery, and other things of everyday use.

Two famous excavated sites are Manda and Shanga, facing each other across Manda Bay, at the end of which may have lain Rhapta. Manda has an immense sea wall of blocks each weighing a ton or more, a sign of a large labor force and the authority to use it. Shanga was occupied by about A.D. 800, and flourished for four hundred years; it was then abandoned. Its congregational mosque was built about A.D. 1050, so in Swahili terms it was then that it was properly "founded." Building in stone followed that in wood about A.D. 950, there being almost two hundred stone buildings dating from the fourteenth century. Building in stone can be taken as a sign of permanent settlement, wealth, and organizational skill.

The first trading settlements were in the north, nearest to Arabia, and then spread southward as the ocean trade developed. As they became engaged in this trade their occupants became Muslims and so "Swahili," the acceptance of Islam marking a culturally distinct Swahili identity. The flowering of Swahili civilization lasted from then until the sixteenth century. Objects from the earlier sites include Chinese porcelain and local domestic pottery, glass beads from India, glass bottles from Yemen and the Levant, iron tools from India, and copper cosmetic articles from Persia. Local craftsmen contributed inlaid ivory and ebony furniture, carved wooden doors, and much silver- and ivory-work. The people wove indigenous cotton and rewove imported silk. Arab travelers of the tenth and later centuries reported words that are recognizable as an early form of KiSwahili and wrote that the local people had sacred kings and domestic slaves. They exported slaves, ivory, ambergris, hides and skins, iron, pearls, rhinoceros horn, rock crystal, and incense, and from the far south gold: these went mainly to Arabia and India, but also to the Middle East, Europe, and China.

The larger towns were places of size, wealth, and splendor, and their standard of living was certainly equal to that of Europe of the time. The famous Arab traveler Muhammed ibn Abdullah ibn Battuta visited the coast in A.D. 1331, and left descriptions of the towns he saw, from Mogadishu in the north, then a Swahili town, to Kilwa in the south. He wrote that the King of Mogadishu walked with sandals, and "over his head they carried a silk canopy, its four poles topped with a golden bird. He wore a sweeping cloak of green Jerusalem stuff, over clothes of Egyptian linen. He had a silk girdle and a large turban" and was preceded by a band of drums, trumpets, and oboes.

Kilwa, in the south of modern Tanzania, is today a place of ruins, but it lasted for over five hundred years. It had three forts, a palace with high buildings extending over five acres, and four mosques, one of which was the finest of the entire African coast. Ibn Battuta called it "one of the most beautiful and well constructed towns in the world." And when the Portuguese conqueror Vasco da Gama visited Kilwa in 1502, his chronicler wrote:

> The city is large and is of good buildings of stone and mortar with terraces, and the houses have much wood work. The city comes down to the shore, and is entirely surrounded by a wall and towers, within which there may be 12,000 inhabitants. The country all around is very luxuriant with many trees and gardens. . . . The streets of the city are very narrow, as the houses are very high, of three and four stories, and one can run along the tops of them upon the terraces, as the houses are very close together: and in the port there were many ships.

This might be written of a Swahili town such as Lamu today. Few European cities of the time were as grand.

The great days of the Swahili were after they had become Muslims until their trade and independence were disturbed and in some places broken by the Portuguese, who arrived on the coast at the very end of the fifteenth century under Vasco da Gama. The Portuguese left detailed accounts of the glories they found, to their astonishment and admiration.

Swahili Chronicles

There are also Swahili accounts that tell of their history from their own perspective. Power, wealth, and the right to control the coastal towns had to be explained and legitimated. This has been done by what are usually referred to as chronicles, documents written by Swahili scholars, usually in Swahili or Arabic and both in Arabic script. The versions that have come down to us are certainly copies of copies. We have no way of knowing what any original myths were like, but that is irrelevant, since myths are constructed not to explain the past but to explain the present as it is thought to have been made by the past, incorporating new materials that appear relevant to the present, and deleting material not thought to be so.

An example is the chronicle of the town of Kilwa, which has written versions in Swahili, Arabic, and Portuguese. It relates the coming to Kilwa of a ship commanded by a prince from Shiraz, in Persia, who was one of seven brothers, the others of whom sailed to other Swahili ports. Kilwa was then said to be almost an island separated from the mainland by a narrow channel of the sea that was above water only at low tide. The prince found the local king and a local Muslim African trader who acted as interpreter. The prince asked to cede the near-island and for the hand of the king's daughter in marriage; the king agreed on payment of as much cloth that could cover the island. It was given to him and he withdrew to the mainland to hunt (probably slaves rather than animals), but planned to return at low tide to kill the prince. The plot was reported to the prince by the interpreter. The prince decided to dig the creek deeper, or in another version, to use Islamic magic to deepen it without human labor. The king returned and, foiled, withdrew to the interior. Later the prince's son visited the king, his maternal grandfather, and married the latter's son's daughter, a proper mother's brother's daughter marriage that legally validated his status as ruler of the town.

These are the essentials of the myth that deals with the settlement of the immigrant merchant line. It gives certain messages. The king was an unclothed hunter and the prince a wealthy merchant with cloth, so there was need for a mediator between them. By being given cloth the king became "civilized" and so able both to trade and have his daughter married to the newcomer as equal in rank. The near-island became a real island, as are most of the sites of the more important Swahili towns. The autochthonous ruler planned to use deceitful warfare, but the prince used morally good Islamic magic, the distinction found today between what are often considered African-derived spirit cults and orthodox Arabian-derived Islam. At first the prince controlled only commerce and lacked political validity, but this was given to his descendants by the later marriage between the two families. The king "hunted" and the prince traded, establishing the pattern of the slave trade when slaves were captured by inland rulers and sold to the Swahili merchants at the coast.

There are similar chronicles for several other towns, all validating the relations between various local African groups and immigrant merchants. The African groups had various economies and were involved in trade: hunters supplied ivory, pastoralists and others of greater political strength supplied other commodities, presumably including slaves. Another well-known Swahili myth tells of the culture hero Fumo Liongo, who is said to have lived as a famous poet of royal ancestry at Shanga on Pate Island until driven to the mainland by intrigues over the succession to the kingdom. There he settled among hunters, the Boni, and led them against Pate. He also married a wife from the pastoralist Oromo people. In other words, he was both an urban poet (the epitome of Swahili civilization) and also associated with simple hunters and with pastoralists, both normally forbidden relationships for Swahili patrician merchants. The three forms of production were merged in him. Fumo Liongo became the ruler and controller of all of them, all needed for a mercantile society, probably at the mythical homeland called Shungwaya. Modern excavations continually produce evidence of elaborate pre-Muslim burial sites that are said to be his. Today these are being destroyed by Muslim fundamentalists who cannot accept that people before Islam could have had kings or built walled towns. But these sad activities do not destroy the reality of history.

Further Reading

Again, the books listed in previous chapters contain material on early Swahili history. In addition, there is a valuable collection of early travelers' accounts:

G. S. P. Freeman-Grenville (ed.). 1962. *The East African Coast: Select Documents from the First to the Earlier Nineteenth Century.* Oxford: Clarendon Press. [The book has many accounts, from many centuries and translated from many languages, that together form a vivid and coherent history of the coast up to the establishment of the Arab colonial sultanate of Zanzibar.]

5

THE OUTSIDE WORLD

The Swahili aroused the envy of other people, and for over four centuries were subjected to overrule first by Portuguese, then by Arabs, and later by other European colonists, mainly British and German. None cared much about Swahili except as people to be exploited for the immense wealth that lay behind them in the interior and which Swahili merchants made available to the rest of the world. East African colonial history has generally been taken from the conquerors' records and we have little from the Swahili side. But we can discern the slow economic impoverishment and political weakening, the development of a wider society whose centers of military power lay elsewhere, and the stubborn persistence of Swahili identity and civilization with occasional periods of local revival.

The Portuguese

The Portuguese arrived in East Africa at the very end of the fifteenth century and stayed for two hundred years. They came to seek spices and the mythical Christian emperor of Ethiopia, Prester John, who would help them fight Islam, and found neither. But they did find ivory, slaves, and especially the gold of Zimbabwe. They

never had more than about two hundred men and women to control the entire coast: soldiers and their mostly Goan and Swahili
wives, various civil officials, and priests and nuns—their aims
included the conversion of local people as subjects of the Portuguese kingdom. They lacked the force to do much except to build
forts, collect customs dues, and make as much money on the side as
they could. They did this by using their powerful Indian Ocean fleet
and by making alliances with various Swahili kings, playing one
against another. In the end the Portuguese devoted most effort to
acquire the gold of Zimbabwe and to ship it to their far eastern colo-
nies to be exchanged for spices. They came as conquerors but soon
came to admire the Swahili as wealthy and educated merchants
whose standard of living was as high or higher than their own.

The Portuguese presence was little more than nominal except
in the south, in Mozambique, where they captured the Swahili
gold trade with Zimbabwe. Apart from some impressive monuments such as the great citadel of Fort Jesus in Mombasa, a few
ruined houses, some loan words in the Swahili language, and local
memory of their cruelty, extortion, and deceit, little has remained.
The Portuguese were the first merchant traders—in fact, virtual
pirates—in the Indian Ocean to use heavily armed ships that could
defeat Arab ships that had long sailed freely across it.

The Portuguese were finally ousted by the Swahili in alliance
with the Arabs of Oman, in southeastern Arabia, who stayed on (as
allies often do) and in 1729 set up the sultanate of Zanzibar with
members of their own royal family as sultans. In 1840 the Omani
Arabs ruled both Oman and Zanzibar with Zanzibar City as the
capital of the single state; they divided it into two states in 1856,
although still under the same ruling line. There remains a close
link between Oman and Zanzibar expressed in migration and family, commercial, and religious ties. KiSwahili is widely spoken in
Oman today.

The Zanzibar Sultanate

The Omani colonial administration at Zanzibar was far more
efficient and ruthless than that of the Portuguese. It lasted from the
early eighteenth until the mid-twentieth centuries and became
feared throughout eastern Africa as far as the Great Lakes and
beyond, although its last seventy years or so were marked by a
decline under the fairly benign control of the British at Zanzibar.

The sultanate was essentially a mercantile state whose rulers, aided by Indian financiers and British advisors, took most of the profitable trade from Swahili hands, leaving them the crumbs. As in so many cases, those who had their power removed became both opponents and at the same time imitators of their conquerors. Swahili took pains to appear as "Arab" as they could. They made claims to having Arabian ancestry and adopted a good deal of Arab and Indian culture. At the same time they kept up a passive resistance expressed largely in terms of dislike, scorn, and covert hostility to the Zanzibar *nouveaux riches*. Most refused to marry their daughters to Arab notables, knowing that to do so would soon lead to loss of their family lands and businesses. Some Swahili did so, mainly in Pemba Island, and came to regret it; they had to wait until the 1964 Zanzibar revolution to regain much of their lands.

Under Sultan Seyyid Barghash ibn Said al-Busaidi Zanzibar reached its apogee in the mid-nineteenth century. As might have been expected, it was soon taken over by European colonial powers, in this case Britain and Germany. During the later nineteenth century, Britain, Germany, France, and the United States competed to take over Zanzibar, a convenient center for the exploitation of both eastern Africa and the western Indian Ocean. Whale oil from the ocean and ivory from the interior were highly valuable for newly capitalist Europe and America: the oil for industrial uses before the large-scale production of mineral oil, and ivory for making piano keys, knife handles, and other household objects for the rising middle classes.

In the end the British and Germans won control over Zanzibar and divided the sultans' domains between themselves by using their superior commercial and naval power to control trade and to shell the sultans' palace. Germany took Tanganyika and Britain took Kenya and Zanzibar itself. In 1918 Britain took over Tanganyika as a League of Nations trust territory. Zanzibar was not a colony but a "protectorate," with a puppet sultan "advised" by a British resident.

Both Britain and Germany realized that the Muslim Swahili were distinct from the many "uncivilized" and illiterate peoples of the African interior. The KiSwahili language was adopted as the official colonial language of East Africa. European concession companies were given large tracts of coastal land in the expectation that the coast would become rich and peaceful. The companies also had to administer the peoples who lived there, but most failed by

The Sultans of Zanzibar

The rulers of the Zanzibar sultanate came from Oman, in southeastern Arabia, and in 1829 drove out the Portuguese colonists who ruled the Swahili coast. The then Imam of Oman, Seyyid Said ibn Sultan, moved his court from Muscat (in Oman) to Zanzibar; he died in 1856, when his domains were divided between his sons, Seyyid Majid ibn Said ruling in Zanzibar and Seyyid Thwain ibn Said in Muscat. Seyyid Majid died in 1870, and later sultans were:

Seyyid Barghash ibn Said, 1870–1888

Seyyid Khalifa ibn Said, 1888–1890

Seyyid Ali ibn Said, 1890–1893

Seyyid Hamed ibn Thwain, 1893–1896

Seyyid Hamoud ibn Mohammad, 1896–1902

Seyyid Ali ibn Hamoud, 1902–1911

Seyyid Khalifa ibn Harub, 1911–1960

Seyyid Abdulla ibn Khalifa, 1960–1962

Seyyid Jamshid ibn Abdulla, 1962–1964

Sultan Jamshid was deposed at the Zanzibar revolution of 1964 and now lives in England.

The title *Seyyid* denotes a direct descendant of the Prophet Muhammad.

their own incompetence. After some years the British realized the greater potential wealth of the interior and dropped their Swahili allies in favor of the inland non-Muslim and often Christian peoples. The Swahili were left to cope for themselves on the coast and saw "progress" passing them by in the rush for the interior. Nothing was done to help them develop a modern productive economy; and their larger ports became mere gateways to the interior, inhabited largely by non-Swahili immigrants. Swahili did what they could to retain their own identity and economy but at the cost of retirement into a passive resistance expressed largely in nostalgia for past glory. There was not much else that they could do.

The Swahili Coast Today

The middle years of the twentieth century were marked by the formal ending of colonial rule in most of Africa, the coming of political independence with the establishment of new nations, and the development of forms of neo-colonialism and control by external bodies such as the World Bank and the International Monetary Fund. The wishes of people such as Swahili were hardly counted as important.

On the Swahili coast there were two overtly political events: the violent and bloody Zanzibar revolution of 1964 and the declarations of independence by Kenya and Tanzania. Both were part of the ending of British overrule but were not greatly welcomed on the coast itself, where the ambiguous relationship between Swahili and the Zanzibar Arabs was of more lasting local significance and has led to much confusion in modern accounts of coastal history. Many writers have simplified this history by seeing it merely as one of European colonial rule oppressing the Arab people of Zanzibar. However, these Arabs were themselves immigrant colonial rulers over the indigenous population. During the sultanate the Arab rulers generally looked down on Swahili, despite adopting their language, and most modern histories have virtually ignored Swahili and placed Zanzibar at the center. Swahili people see the situation differently, as more complex than that of British rule over an oppressed coastal population. In their view, they were the victims of Zanzibar rather than of British colonialism. "History" depends on where one stands.

The new postcolonial rulers, especially in Kenya, have used Swahili as scapegoats for many of their failures. They have largely ignored them in development schemes, educational facilities, government appointments, and many other areas of modern government. In the later years of the twentieth century Swahili land was taken from them for resettlement of people from the overcrowded interior and for profitable building by non-Swahili entrepreneurs. At local levels of administration the larger Swahili towns are almost always governed by non-Swahili and non-Muslim officials, many of whom appear to see their tenure at the coast as both a way of extending the lands and wealth of the immigrants from the interior and of making money for themselves.

The last century saw deep political changes in Swahili society. The sultanate's overrule destroyed much of the former independence of the coastal towns and put them under the control of governors (liwali) and lesser officials, almost all of them Zanzibar Arabs. The near-destruction of the Swahili mercantile economy by favoring Arab and Indian traders and setting up customs tariffs on exports and imports led to the weakening of the patrician elite. Swahili tried, with little success, to build political parties to restore coastal autonomy. With national independence in the 1960s they were joined, with various degrees of enthusiasm, by Arab representatives who wished to bring back their own formerly superior position. The first serious movement, known as Mwambao (The Coast), never got very far as it contained too many internal conflicts between Swahili and Arabs. The same happened with the Kenya African Democratic Union under the Mijikenda leader Ronald Ngala, which lost out to the more widely supported Kenya African National Union led by Jomo Kenyatta. In Zanzibar there appeared new political parties for the elections held by the British. After the British left in 1963, Zanzibar retained a constitutional monarchy under the young Sultan Jamshid ibn Abdullah. The 1964 Zanzibar revolution ended the monarchy and brought a dictatorial government of mostly immigrant African leaders who themselves oppressed the local population. Zanzibar is still the scene of vicious elections between the same elements. In 1964 Zanzibar was absorbed into Tanzania under President Nyerere, and Swahili lost power and position everywhere on the coast.

Swahili self-consciousness, however much ignored by the central national governments, is in their own eyes proper, legitimate, and successful. Their basic strategy has been to ensure that Swahili identity and pride are maintained by the reflowering of Swahili civilization, cultural and religious exclusivity, and emphasis on customary moral norms. A visit to Swahili towns may give an impression of unchanging places inhabited by old-fashioned people stuck in old-fashioned ways. This impression would be far from reality. All Swahili merchants, fishermen and women, and craftsmen from boatbuilders to sandal makers, are extremely competent in the modern world, fully aware of the problems of competition and exchange, and experienced in keeping an informal, concealed, but fairly effective control over their local administrators. A visitor from the new "global" world of late-capitalism may have the impression of quiet people going about their everyday ways, their women veiled and most men wearing long white robes and attending mosques several times a day. These same polite and reserved people have a very clear view of their visitors and the countries from which they come. Many households have radio and videos; their members are literate and read newspapers; their Friday mosque services include discussion of outside events affecting them. As for "globalization," for people whose ancestors traded with Egypt and India over a thousand years ago, it is hardly anything new.

They also know the importance in the modern world of a central feature of their civilization, literate education. Traditional Swahili education is much prized, based on the inculcation of Muslim values, learning, and religious beliefs. Modern education in the rest of East Africa is secular, generally Christian, and so unwelcome to Muslims. Swahili are not fools and see clearly that their future requires both forms of education. The one ensures the retention of their identity and the other enables their children to make their ways in the outside modern world. Many Swahili children whom I know attend both kinds of school, making their working days long and exhausting, but they persevere in doing so. The government helps only a handful to continue to higher education. The policies of their governments (especially Kenya) include removing power from the Swahili community, so that there is the paradox of these modern independent countries deliberately ignoring the potential of part of their educated population for narrow political and sectarian reasons.

Since the late 1960s, in Zanzibar, the royal palaces and the famous British administrative offices of cast iron pillars and silver staircases, the Beit-el-Ajaib, the "House of Wonders," have been turned into offices for the Zanzibar ruling party and into tourist attractions. In Mombasa the former British High Court is part of the Fort Jesus Museum, and the great fort itself is neither a Portuguese fort nor a British prison, but the Coast Museum headquarters. Throughout the coast the red flag of Zanzibar no longer flies on public buildings, and the public clocks no longer show Zanzibar time, with one o'clock marking the first hours of daylight and nighttime, but the standard time of the rest of the world. As well as that world, the relics, ruins, and the skills of crafts, music, and poetry remain significant for understanding the present as merely a phase in the long Swahili history.

Further Reading

Most of the previously listed books have material on Swahili history. Others include:

J. M. Gray. 1962. *A History of Zanzibar from the Middle Ages to 1856*. London: Oxford University Press. [A straightforward political history.]

Jonathon Glassman. 1995. *Feasts and Riot: Revelry, Rebellion, and Popular Consciousness on the Swahili Coast, 1856–1888*. Portsmouth, NH: Heinemann. [An excellent account of the local reaction to German colonial rule in a Tanganyika town.]

Abdul M. H. Sheriff and E. Ferguson (eds.). 1991. *Zanzibar under Colonial Rule.* London: Currey. [Good account of the growth of class stratification.]

Frederick Cooper. 1987. *On the African Waterfront: Urban Disorder and the Transformation of Work in Colonial Mombasa.* New Haven: Yale University Press. [A detailed study of modern industrialization in an ancient Swahili city.]

John Middleton and Jane Campbell. 1965. *Zanzibar, Its History and Its Politics.* London: Oxford University Press. [Zanzibar on the eve of the 1964 revolution.]

M. F. Lofchie. 1965. *Zanzibar: Background to Revolution.* Princeton: Princeton University Press. [An account of political parties and relations in the 1960s.]

6

TOWNSPEOPLE

Swahili people have lived in towns from the eighth and ninth centuries, when they accepted Islam and built the first mosques. A mosque is the center of a Swahili town, and a town is properly founded *(-buni)* only by the building of its mosque; before that, it is merely a cluster of buildings without identity. Most Islamic towns elsewhere in the world are defined by having a central market and public baths as well as a central mosque, but this is not so of Swahili towns. Many of their towns are architecturally unique, there being no others like them in Africa or the Islamic world beyond it.

All Swahili settlements are called by their inhabitants *miji* (singular *mji*), the everyday word for towns. Each one is slightly different from others in both appearance and in composition. The larger Swahili settlements are highly urban, most of them with permanent houses densely set in paved and drained streets. Not all their settlements are urban in this physical sense, and we should distinguish two main types: I call them stone-towns and country-towns, to refer to their more obvious differences in architecture and pattern of streets and open spaces.

The stone-towns are those of the merchants, living in close-knit areas mainly of large coral block houses; many of these towns once had surrounding walls. The country-towns are those of fishermen and farmers, and most are straggling villages of less permanent materials. We must follow Swahili usage and not distinguish them too rigidly: they represent the two ends of a single continuum along which lie all the towns. Inhabitants of stone-towns have engaged in intercontinental trade between Africa and Asia, and until the end of the nineteenth century depended on slave labor. Inhabitants of country-towns neither engaged in long-distance trade nor kept slaves and have provided food and labor to the stone-towns. In return stone-town people provided them with protection and goods from the Asian trade. The interdependence of all these local communities up and down the coast has always been a feature of Swahili society.

Domestic Architecture

Swahili houses, *nyumba*, are rectangular; some are of two or even three stories in height; all have complex internal layouts. They are the most important items of property in this mercantile society; they are places for trade exchange, everyday living, weddings, births, and deaths. They can last for many generations. They are similar, to almost the smallest detail, to those of ruined towns of many centuries ago, showing a remarkable continuity of culture and domestic organization. Swahili people see stone-towns as centers of Islamic learning, literacy, and poetry, and of mercantile enterprise and wealth. Their streets are places of commerce, conversation, evil spirits, and the everyday in all its impiety and pollution. Their mosques and houses, on the other hand, are places of purity set within the dirt of the surrounding streets. Former town walls were both for protection and to mark the boundary between Swahili and non-Swahili peoples and between the world of Islam and the non-Islamic wilderness outside it.

The patrician stone-towns are so called because their main buildings are made of blocks of coral, known locally as "stones," *mawe*. Most of these houses are on the northern part of the coast, in towns such as Pate and Lamu. Those of Mombasa Old Town are mostly so-called "Indian" or "verandah" houses, tall buildings of several floors with a single apartment on each floor and without the traditional internal arrangement of rooms. In a town such as Pate, the buildings are of one story only, with palm-leaf roofs; in Lamu and a few other places where land is in short supply, they are built upwards and most are of three stories, with flat roofs.

The coral used for building is of two kinds. One, the heavy rag, is used for walls. The other, taken from under the watermark on the coral, is soft and easily workable and used for lintels and other carvings; after a little time it becomes hard and durable. Ceilings are of mangrove poles, limited in length to three meters, so that rooms cannot be wider and are typically long and narrow. The external walls are thick, often as much as two meters; internal walls are thinner. Once built, the outer walls may last for two or three centuries if cared for by regular cleaning and lime washing. Many stone houses of Pate and Lamu, for example, are certainly this old, and those of ruined settlements may be much older and often still standing.

These houses have no windows, and light comes from the central courtyard. On the street side, each house has a double door of elaborately carved and decorated wood. The door is set inside a porch, *daka*; on the porch are side benches of lime cement for visitors to sit and talk with the house owner. The great door repels the outside world, and with the high walls marks a clear boundary between the street and the household. The house's central courtyard, *kiwanda*, is used for general household activity and storage. In former times female slaves would sleep at one corner of it. Family life takes place in the rooms behind the courtyard, gained by steps and separated from it by a waist-high dividing wall.

The living rooms are long transverse galleries *(msana)*, each as wide as the house and three meters (the length of the mangrove poles used for ceilings) in depth. The ceilings are high, so keeping the galleries cool. There are either two or three galleries, one behind the other, each a step higher than the one in front. In larger houses there is first the "lower gallery" *(msana wa tini)*, behind it the "upper gallery" *(msana wa yuu)*, and behind that the "inside" or "inner gallery" *(ndani)*. Small houses have only the lower and the inner galleries. The inner gallery is the room of the household head and his wife; the upper gallery is for other family members; and the lower gallery is used for invited visitors and casual conversation. There are no separate bedrooms: beds are merely placed at the ends of the galleries, behind curtains. Furniture is simple, mainly chairs, low stools, and cushions; there are no tables.

The back wall of the inner gallery has two doors. One leads to a room called *nyumba ya kati*, "the middle of the house," even though it is at one of the rear corners. It is at the "middle" because it is used for various sacred activities, mainly for seclusion of women

Swahili House Furniture

There are virtually no accounts of the interior of Swahili houses, presumably because few non-Swahili visitors were ever invited into them (visitors were more impressed by the elegance of Swahili clothing). Under the Zanzibar sultanate and with the growing importance of Indian traders and financiers, Swahili patricians in particular adopted Indian furnishings. Much of "Swahili furniture" is in fact made by Indian craftsmen, either in India or locally on the East African coast.

The walls of grander houses were once hung with imported and locally woven silk and cotton tapestries. Few have lasted until today, but the pegs for hanging them are still visible on house walls. The main pieces of furniture were and still are bedsteads, both simple Swahili beds and more elaborate and painted Indian ones (wealthy people used silver steps to climb into them); many types of chairs from those of ebony and ivory to embroidered couches and to ordinary wooden chairs and stools; most houses have many cushions and rugs; tables and closets are rarely used. All houses are lit by oil lamps and, today in the larger towns, by electricity.

during menstruation and childbirth, and for washing the corpses of family members. The other door leads to the family bathroom and pit latrine (there are others in the courtyard). There is also a special guest suite, *sabule*, with its own staircase leading directly from the courtyard and so totally separated from the family galleries.

All stone houses follow this basic plan. The galleries always face north, towards Mecca; prevailing winds and rains come from the south, and so the galleries are protected from them. Since street entrances can face in any direction, due to layouts of the streets, houses may have to be built with winding staircases so that the galleries face north.

The inner gallery and the main bathroom behind it have elaborate plastered designs, which are given frequent lime washings. The rear wall of this gallery has small alcoves or niches (*zidaka*) along it, in which are placed precious and beautiful objects and heirlooms. Other galleries and the courtyard are kept lime washed but are not decorated. The room called "the middle of the house" is not lime washed, as it is a place of continual pollution. There is a clear link between purity, plastering, and lime washing, the more pure rooms being the most elaborately plastered.

The end of the upper gallery of a patrician house. It is used as a bedroom, a dividing curtain being hung from the bar near the ceiling. The high and narrow ceiling is made of mangrove poles laid transversely—their limit of length is only about 3 meters. At the end is a small decorative alcove and an elaborate plastered wall decoration kept lime washed for beauty and purity. *(Nancy Nooter)*

The houses of country-towns are built on approximately the same plan, but with lower and inner rooms instead of galleries. Plastering is not feasible, but low, outside coral walls are at least lime washed. These houses have no carved doors and are typically surrounded by palm-leaf fences as boundaries.

Sacred Buildings

Both stone-towns and country-towns have mosques, which vary in size from immense ornamented buildings to small, simple, and unadorned structures. A mosque, *msikiti*, is different in plan from an ordinary dwelling house. From the outside a mosque may look like a large house, but mosques have large windows, and their doors are kept open; inside is an open, mat-covered space for prayer, and at the Mecca end is an alcove known as *qibla*. Some mosques have rows of pillars to support a wide roof of mangrove poles; several very large ones have arches and galleries set on side pillars. All have ablution places located outside the side doors. Thus, a mosque must have a well or other source of clean water. Stone benches are usually built along one or more sides on which men sit and discuss daily events. Mosques are sacred places and not open to non-Muslims. Muslim schools, *madrasa*, are attached to most mosques, forming with them single complexes of Islamic learning and piety.

Cemeteries are typically set at northern and southern ends of towns. Stones mark the graves, often with wooden roofs over them, in particular those of religious scholars considered to be saints. In the streets of most towns are stone tombs of saints who once lived in the particular town, carefully preserved from destruction. They are usually destinations of pilgrimage, often from long distances.

There are no lived-in palaces today. The sultans of Zanzibar had several in and near Zanzibar City, but since the 1964 revolution the Zanzibar government has used them for other purposes. The last-occupied Swahili palace was that of the indigenous ruler of Zanzibar Island, the Mwenye Mkuu, "the Great Owner" of the Hadimu people; the ruins are at Dunga, in the center of the island. There are also ruins of palaces at Gedi, Pate, and especially at the southern town of Kilwa, where there is a set of immense buildings that fell into ruins during the eighteenth century.

Country-towns

The largest number of Swahili country-towns is in the islands of Zanzibar and Pemba, occupied mainly by the groups known as WaHadimu and WaPemba respectively. Most are along the eastern shores, set back from the beaches, their rectangular houses crowded together in clusters separated by spaces of sand and coral. They are typically built on the outcrops of continually occupied and fertilized soil, which rise up like islands from the flat coral rag. Each town consists of settlements spread out over one or two miles, with a single central congregational mosque in the parent settlement of the town from which the outlying units are said to have spread. Towns vary greatly in size, from a few hundred people to several thousand; the average is about 1,500 people. Most are long settled, and there is little spare land left these days for building new ones. A town is surrounded by its townlands of several square miles and marked off from neighboring townlands by boundary trees, usually small areca palms that grow the nuts used in chewing with betel. These towns are economically dependent on exploiting both the lagoons and the open sea as well as their gardens and fields. Some specialize in fruit growing, a few in mangrove cutting, and all supply seasonal labor to nearby clove plantations. Until the 1964 revolution the sultanate government reserved the clove plantations for Arab landowners, and Hadimu and Pemba people were not allowed to grow cloves.

Country-town houses are made either of coral blocks or more usually of earth and lime walls, with roofs of coconut palm leaves or corrugated iron sheets. There is always a central town mosque, small shops, washing places, public latrines, and places for sitting and mending nets and sails. Double outrigger and smaller canoes are drawn up on the beaches or anchored in the lagoons.

Small gardens, *mashamba* (singular *shamba*), are set among the houses. They may be fertilized and at times irrigated, and used for growing household crops, fruit trees, and bananas (which are not counted as trees but as ordinary plants). Coconut palms are planted anywhere there is room for them. Beyond are the fields, *konde*, on which people grow grains, cassava, and sesame (for its oil), a laborious task in coral areas where there is little deep soil. In all country-towns fertile and watered land is scarce, but the pattern of closely and carefully cultivated gardens makes the most efficient use of it; certainly no patch of good soil is ever unused. Small white flags are set in most of the stony areas, to mark the shrines for the many spirits that live outside the settlements.

Outside the townlands proper are many swampy areas for growing rice, the preferred staple, clumps of wild trees including many kinds of palms, and stretches of grass for the few cattle kept. The impression is that of wide landscapes with scattered fields and trees surrounding the islands of higher soil on which are the houses, coconut palms, and lush gardens. The settlements do not face inland but towards the sea, always visible through the coconut palms.

Country-towns are usually divided into constituent villages, *vijiji* (literally, "little towns"). The living spaces of a village are together referred to by the word *kiambo*, best translated by the loose word "home." It is occupied by the family groups who "own" the small clusters of houses called *vitongo* (singular *kitongo*) and also by their tenants, who are distant kin from other towns who come there usually because there is some spare garden space for them.

These productive units of a country-town are linked to two other patterns, one of space and the other of descent and kinship.

A fishing and farming village (country-town) of the people of southern Zanzibar island, those usually known as Hadimu. The man wears a white gown, *kanzu*, and an embroidered white cap, *kofia*. The houses have limewashed and painted coral block walls and roofs of corrugated iron and palm-leaf thatch. Coconut palms and bananas are planted wherever there is room among the houses. (*Photo by author*)

All towns are divided into spatial units called *mitaa* (singular *mtaa*). The word is used in several ways but always for a part or piece of a whole: a mtaa never stands alone as a single place. Every country-town is divided into two mitaa, usually translated as "moieties." Moieties are separated by the central congregational mosque and often also by an unbuilt stretch of grass or sand. The main feature of this dualism is the opposition between moieties. Each moiety usually has its own football and dance teams; they compete fiercely against each other but merge when competing against other towns. The dance companies are known as *beni* (from the English word, band) and are highly popular. There are ritually charged occasions such as the New Year, known as *mwaka*, "year," or Nauruz (a Persian word), when in some towns the young men of one moiety fight with swords against those of the other. (See chapter 12 for a discussion of the Swahili calendar.) Until recently these were by no means token games, and many men were wounded or even killed. These and other New Year rites bring about the purification of an entire town from the pollution of the previous year. Opposition is actively played out between the moieties, and the violence "cools" both of them as parts of a single whole.

Towns are also divided into smaller units than moieties. These are also known as *mitaa*, and may be called in English "wards" or "quarters." A ward is the basic spatial unit of a town or village: people say that they live in a particular ward, which has its own name and boundaries, its residential area holding several vitongo. Each ward is under the authority of its head, the "big man of the ward," *mkubwa wa mtaa*. He is responsible for order within it, for settlement of personal disputes, and for controlling the acceptance of would-be tenants from elsewhere. He is also keeper of the "purse" of the ward, made up of tenants' fees and fines for ill behavior between members. The ward heads of a town are together known as Watu Wanne, "The Four Men," and form its traditional government, which provides the basis for present-day councils. A ward is occupied by a cluster of cognatic kin and is a corporate territorial group. This means that it is assumed to be permanent even though its members live and die and new ones are born; it has its own head or manager; and it is considered a single legal unit to be represented in law cases by its head.

The people who live in a country-town are thus members of villages, "homes," moieties, and wards. Each of these is relevant in a different situation, whether productive, residential, political, or legal. People are also members of kinship groups, based on descent and shared ancestry. Members of country-towns reckon descent cognatically, through both men and women from a common ancestor, either male or female. Among the WaHadimu and WaPemba the main descent group is known as *ukoo* (plural *koo*); each ukoo is linked to a particular town and its members are known as its owners, *wenyeji*. Some of its inhabitants are tenants from other towns, usually being cousins of the "owners." The members of any single ukoo are thus scattered throughout many towns, but they always remain conscious of their particular ancestral town. The same applies to all country-towns on the coast, although many use different words for the Hadimu ukoo.

A ukoo is the largest of several kinds of descent groups, all relevant in different situations of residence and production. A ukoo is divided into groups known generally as *matumbo* (singular *tumbo*, "womb" or "stomach"). Members of a single tumbo typically form the occupants of a single ward and share its land. An even smaller group is the *mlango* (plural *milango*), "gate" or "door," as through it its members may "pass into" the ukoo itself. Members of a tumbo or mlango occupy a single kitongo and share its gardens. As cognatic groups, none of these kin groups are corporate.

Stone-towns

Most stone-towns are situated on small islands nestled inside wide creeks for protection against the force of the ocean and also against raiders from the interior; others are on the shores of creeks or estuaries themselves. All are mercantile ports-of-trade and need good and safe harbors. The centers of most of them consist of long-lasting stone buildings surrounded by smaller houses of palm fronds and other impermanent materials. The larger stone-towns may contain as many as twenty mosques, including a central or congregational mosque at the town center. The stone-built houses are owned by the patrician merchant families, who are only a minority of the total coastal population. Most of the other houses are occupied by the poor and the descendants of slaves. In most of these towns there are also Arab and Indian families living in modern concrete-block houses outside the patrician core.

Urbanity (utamaduni) is a central notion in Swahili civilization and is used especially in association with stone-towns. It means living graciously and courteously and also refers to the careful marking of spatial distinctions. Every town is divided into public spaces and private spaces. Public spaces are the streets, jetties, food markets, and spaces for dancing, rope making, and other activities shared by men and women. They are also open to visitors and strangers. Private spaces are mosques, houses, and small gardens. Domestic houses are places of privacy: within them women are unveiled; outside them they are veiled to conceal their physical and moral privacy from the eyes of men unrelated to them. Mosques are not private in the same sense, but are sacred and almost all are limited to Muslim men. Most men and women wear traditional clothing outside their houses, with leather sandals. Sandals are removed when entering a house or mosque, which are places of purity (*usafi*); outside they protect a person from the material and symbolic dirt of the streets. Slaves were not permitted to wear sandals, robes, caps, or veils when working (modern tourists often walk barefoot, and local people are insulted by such bad manners).

All stone-towns are divided into moieties and wards, both referred to as mitaa. Until the abolition of slavery the moieties of probably all stone-towns were inhabited by patricians, their slaves living with them in the patrician houses. With the abolition of slavery, the limits of most towns were widened and outlying "suburbs" of ex-slaves and their descendants formed new residential moieties. An example is the town of Lamu: the original patrician moieties were known as Mkomani and Mtamuini. After abolition they were amalgamated as one, known as Mkomani (so many slaves left that the original two were only partly inhabited). A new moiety called Langoni (at the gate) was established for ex-slaves and other nonpatricians and became the opposing moiety, as it remains today.

The largest town of all, Mombasa, is likewise divided into two moieties, which are called "confederations" in the literature. Each contains several descent groups, each with its own name, and are together known as "The Three Tribes," Thelatha Taifa, and "The Nine Tribes," Tisa Taifa. They do not comprise strictly territorial groups, but most of The Three Tribes occupy the northern part of Mombasa Island, and their members are together known as WaMvita, "People of Mombasa," and The Nine Tribes occupy the southern part and their members are together known as WaKilindini, "People of the Deep Harbor." Each cluster has outlying subgroups on the mainland. Each cluster is under the formal authority

A residential street in Lamu town. It shows the walls of Swahili patricians' "stone" houses with a bridge over the street so that the women of the houses can pass between them without being publicly seen unveiled. The two women here wear the black veils and gowns *(buibui)* of ordinary Swahili women when outside their homes. *(Justine Baruch)*

of an elected official, the Tamim. The two groups of twelve tribes—really subclans—were the original mercantile groups of the town; today, although unimportant politically, they are still relevant in the selection of marriage partners.

Stone-town wards are not occupied by clusters of kin, as are country-town wards. The stone-town wards are merely blocks of houses separated by streets and alleys; these blocks are themselves divided by streets, which do not represent residential boundaries. Wards are named by believed places of origins or by occupations of their original inhabitants. They have little function except to provide addresses, and are not corporate as are those of country-towns.

Swahili Clothing

Everyday clothing for women consists of a pair of square pieces of cotton or silk known as *leso* or *khanga*: one is used as a wrapper and the other to cover the head and shoulders. Today they are made in China and India, and better quality ones are made in The Netherlands and Britain. They have colored designs and usually proverbs or mottoes, often political or erotic. Women also wear long gowns and veils *(buibui)* outside their houses, some being colored and most being black, introduced from Zanzibar during early Arab colonial rule. The veils usually cover all but the eyes; they are opened and closed by the woman's hand so that she can cover or expose as much of her face as she wishes. There are several remote settlements where women are unveiled. Younger women working in commercial or government offices usually wear veils, but they are small and do not cover the face. Women wear leather sandals when in the streets. Inside their houses women remove their black gowns and veils, and wear modern European style dresses and other informal clothing. Early Portuguese accounts emphasized the colorful elegance of the patrician women who wore Chinese silks and golden jewelry. Slave women wore only black wrappers and no sandals.

Clothing for men when not working in the fields and gardens comprises a long embroidered white robe, *kanzu*, and a round cap of white cloth with silk designs, *kofia*, of which there are many patterns. Men also wear sandals in the streets. A bridegroom wears the traditional ornate patrician clothing of a sleeveless colored waistcoat, *kisibau*, over the *kanzu*, a turban, *kilemba*, and dagger and sword. Today men working in offices usually wear a European-style jacket over the *kanzu*.

Patricians reckon descent in the patrilineal line. They divide themselves into what may be called subclans whose members claim to have come from ancestral clans in Arabia. The historical accuracy of these claims is very uncertain. A clan is thus dispersed

A Swahili woman wearing a black veil, worn by women when in public places. The veil is held by one hand and so the wearer can move it up or down to expose less or more of her face and eyes. *(Dominique Malaquais)*

among many subclans in both Africa and Arabia. It has no head (that is not so in the case of Arab subclans of Arabian ancestry) nor formal council; nor is it corporate. A typical stone-town has a dozen or more subclans of different ancestries, there being perhaps from fifty to a hundred clans represented along the entire coast. People refer to clans and subclans as kabila or taifa; both are terms that refer to large territorial or ethnic groups of any kind.

A patrician subclan is divided into lineages, usually referred to as matumbo or milango. These are the corporate groups of a stone-town; they own the great stone houses and were the basic groups involved in long-distance trade. They are often referred to as *shirika*, a "company" in the sense of a close-knit business. Each is under the formal authority of a senior male.

The subclans of a town are ranked, the main criteria being its wealth and its claimed date of immigration from Arabia, however dubious such claims may be. An example is from Lamu, where

Lamu, a Stone-town

Lamu is the main town on the northern Kenya coast, with some 15,000 inhabitants today but only half that number a century ago. It stretches for about a mile along the southeastern shore of a wide creek about two miles from the sea itself. It is about a quarter of a mile across, backed by miles of sand dunes that act as filters for rainwater for the town's wells.

The wide *usita wa pwani*, "the street of the shore," has many jetties and landing places, and is backed by a line of large twentieth century "Indian" or "verandah" houses used mainly for government and commercial offices. Parallel behind it runs the long *usita wa mui*, "the street of the town," with stone houses used as small shops. From it many small unnamed streets of stone living houses run uphill to the dunes behind, with many side streets, alleys, deserted house sites used as gardens, and some twenty small mosques.

The town is divided into two moieties. The northern part (nearest to Mecca), known as Mkomani (the place of the hyphaene palm), is the original patrician half of the town; the southern part, Langoni (at the gate), contains the small houses of nonpatricians, main modern concrete block houses owned by Arabs, the fort (now a museum), the great "Mosque of the Sacred Meadows" (see the photo on page 118), the hospital, police station, electricity plant, and tourist hotels.

The streets are too narrow for automobiles, transport being by donkeys, and even pedal bicycles are forbidden.

The seafront at Lamu town. It shows the *usita wa pwani* "the street of the beach," with the large colonial "Indian" or "verandah" houses of the early twentieth century and today used as government and commercial offices, hotels, and coffee shops. The street, a hundred yards or so wide, is always filled with people waiting patiently for sailing ferries, drinking coffee and discussing political, religious, and social matters, or merely idling while passing the time of day. *(Justine Baruch)*

there are twelve recognized subclans with long histories of living in the town, and half a dozen or so socially inferior ethnic groups of many kinds. At the top are the Wenye Moi, "Owners of the Town"; then come the Banu Lamii, "Children of Lamu"; then the Watu Wakuu, "Great People"; and then the Wenye Ezi, "Owners of Power." Each category includes all those above it. Together they form the traditional town government and consider themselves to be the "true patricians," *waungwana wa haki* or *waungwana wa yumbe*, "patricians of the government." There follow three subclans recognized as being the longest settled of all, but they do not claim Arabian ancestry. In the past they performed various ritual duties but have little everyday authority. All these fifteen subclans are classed together as WaAmu, "Lamuans." Other subclans follow whose members are not patricians, the first five classed with the WaAmu to form the Watu wa Lamu, "People of Lamu." Finally, there are three categories of non-Swahili immigrants, some of whose ancestors arrived many generations ago and others who are recent arrivals. The former are respected, while the latter are unpopular and distrusted.

Further Reading

There are several accounts of individual towns. The most usable include:

Patricia Caplan. 1975. *Choice and Constraint in a Swahili Community.* London: Oxford University Press. [Mafia Island.]

Marc Swartz. 1991. *The Way the World Is.* Berkeley: University of California Press. [Mombasa.]

A. H. J. Prins. 1965. *Sailing from Lamu: A Study of Maritime Culture in Islamic East Africa.* Assen, Netherlands: Van Gorcum. [Lamu.]

A. H. M. el-Zein. 1974. *The Sacred Meadows: A Structural Analysis of Religious Symbolism in an East African Town.* Evanston, IL: Northwestern University Press. [Lamu.]

Jonathan Glassman. 1995. *Feasts and Riot: Revelry, Rebellion, and Popular Consciousness on the Swahili Coast, 1856–1888.* Portsmouth, NH: Heinemann. [Pangani.]

John Middleton. 1961. *Land Tenure in Zanzibar.* London: HMSO. [The country-towns of Zanzibar and Pemba.]

H. DeBlij. 1968. *Mombasa: An African City.* Evanston, IL: Northwestern University Press. [Mombasa.]

Abdul Sheriff. 1995. *The History and Conservation of the Zanzibar Stonetown.* London: James Currey. [Zanzibar City.]

Accounts of Swahili architecture include:

J. S. Kirkman. 1964. *Men and Monuments on the East African Coast.* London: Butterworth.

Mark Horton and John Middleton. 2000. *The Swahili.* Oxford: Blackwell.

U. Ghaidan. 1975. *Lamu: A Study of a Swahili Town.* Nairobi: East African Literature Bureau.

7

RANK AND FAMILY

Besides organization by locality and descent, people of Swahili towns bond themselves by rank and by association. These are linked in everyday life: people live and work as members of families and households and place one another by degrees of social stratification, formally rigid yet permeable in everyday actuality.

Rank and Status

Swahili people recognize differences of rank or degree, to a greater extent in the stone-towns than in the country-towns. The merchants of the stone-towns are generally classed as waungwana (usually translated as patricians). They are not landed aristocrats; they put their wealth into elegance of everyday living rather than into land. They define themselves and are considered by other people as the possessors of the moral and personal quality known as uungwana (gentility).

The patricians arrange themselves in an order of ranks, for which Swahili use the term *daraja*. The word means both "a step of a ladder" and "a bridge," and so refers to movement from one position to another. It also implies that such movement is an integral part of claiming rank of any kind: nothing is immutable. The word "degree" might perhaps be better than rank, being less marked by formal difference in clothing or standard of living, a difference that carries the implication of "good" or "bad" moral behavior as well as ethnic origin; but "rank" is so often used in English that we may retain it.

We may see Swahili society as its members see it, in the form of a pyramid. At the top are the patricians of the stone-towns; at the bottom were the slaves until the twentieth century, and since then the descendants of slaves, the wazalia, "those born to the country" or "those born to the household." This term is rarely used as it is thought offensive. In between are many nonpatrician groups and categories. There has always been movement of members of these intermediary categories between the coastal towns, for several reasons: improvement of one's career, fear of sickness or witchcraft, and attempts to increase personal rank by claiming membership of an ethnic group higher than one's own. For example, in the twentieth century large numbers of Bajun fishermen moved south from their northern settlements and then claimed "Arab" ancestry in order to pay fewer taxes, to be counted as Arab in law cases, and to be allocated rice instead of sorghum when food was rationed during the Second World War. The British decennial censuses almost always showed immense changes in ethnic affiliation due to moves of this kind.

Kings and Queens

Almost every stone-town had at one time or another a king, *mfalme*, or queen, *malkia*. Most of them reigned rather than ruled, as their powers were rarely very great. Most were kings, as records show only twenty-five regnant queens over six or seven centuries. Many queens may be mythical, "mother-founders" of their towns. Some may have been widows—since royal marriages were between very close cousins, especially paternal parallel cousins, kings and queens, whether the latter were regnant or not, would have been close kin of the same subclans, their authority linked by birth and not necessarily terminated on the death of the king. Certainly some queens were rulers in their own right. Kings and queens were sacred beings, their physical gender being unimportant: they were regarded as spiritually and symbolically "male."

Kings and queens are reported from early centuries, especially by Arab and Portuguese observers. These left several vivid accounts of them, the most detailed by the famous Arab traveler Ibn Battuta. The Portuguese assumed that they were essentially similar to European rulers of the period, even if not as powerful and of course non-Christian, and made alliances with them against common enemies (usually other kings along the coast).

The kings had certain duties. One was to act as the hub of their towns' various networks of commercial relations that were established to ensure orderly purchase and sale of trade commodities. Kings allotted visiting traders to the merchants and were themselves traders in their own right. Another duty was to represent their towns vis-à-vis foreign visitors and traders, such as the Portuguese; the more splendid and flamboyant they were, the greater was the reputation of their towns as safe places to visit and with which to trade. Their sacredness was important: they stood for the glory and morality of their towns, were given sacred regalia (drums, elaborate chairs, great horns, special clothes—including scarlet cloth from India) and were set apart from ordinary citizens. Only a few seem to have exercised much authority, and most were largely figureheads: legends of their cruelty and possession of symbols of pomp and sacredness do not necessarily refer to any real material power. The last king, the Mwenye Mkuu, the "Great Owner," of the WaHadimu people of Zanzibar Island, died in 1873; all others had been weakened and destroyed by the sultans of Zanzibar. All that remains of them today are the ruins of their great palaces and a few regalia in local museums.

Internal Government

Almost every town has its traditional form of internal government, although it is ultimately controlled by the modern central governments. There are two main traditional types of town government: one is in the northern coast and the other is to the south from the Mrima coast to Mozambique. It has been suggested that the southern type is the older or original pattern and the northern one is linked to the influx of clans from Arabia. This cannot yet be demonstrated. In both types there was almost always a recognized king or queen. There has never been a single Swahili polity or state with a single ruler, unless we count their unwilling subjection by the sultanate of Zanzibar, which forced them into a single political unit.

In the southern towns most forms of government were in the hands of elected officials who were given titles modeled on believed

Persian or other Asian systems. They were under the formal authority of single heads, with many local titles, of which *jumbe* (a term still used for a village headman), *shomvi*, or *diwani* were the most common. Lesser officials included *waziri*, "chief minister," mwenye mkuu, "great owner or chief elder," *akida*, "war leader," *mataka*, "judge," and many others. All had their own regalia and privileges, wore special robes, and were given elaborate funerals. They worked their way up from lower to higher ranks by giving large feasts—they had to be wealthy and they seem mostly to have been merchants. We know little of how they actually governed, but their responsibilities seem largely to have been devoted to maintaining formal patterns of ranking between patricians, nonpatricians, and slaves of various kinds. Their towns were very small and their authority formal and personal rather than sanctioned by much force. Accounts of them begin long after they had been weakened by the Portuguese and the Zanzibar sultans, and so we have only a shadow knowledge of them.

In the northern part of the coast the patricians possessed greater authority, and until the end of the nineteenth century only their moieties provided the personnel for a stone-town's government, each moiety ruling its town alternately for four years. Whereas in the southern towns political authority was largely by wealth, in the northern ones it was by ancestry.

The country-towns have had, and still have to some extent, small-scale democratic forms of government, of which the most widespread appears to be forms of council. In rural Zanzibar, for example, each town still has its council, known as Watu Wanne, "The Four Men," together with an elected headman, a central-government-appointed representative known as the *sheha*, and the ritual leader (separate from local mosque controllers) known as *mzale* or *mvyale*, almost always a woman, whose task is to control the evil spirits of the neighborhood.

The Zanzibar sultanate appointed its own governors (liwali) and lesser administrators of towns and stretches of coast. They seem always to have been kin of the Arab sultans and were generally disliked and distrusted as representatives of what Swahili considered a conquering colonial power. The liwali kept their positions until the Zanzibar revolution of 1964. The sultans also appointed judges, always Arabs, and commanders of the sultans' troops stationed up and down the coast, usually Baluchi mercenaries who for many years were under the command of a British general, Sir Lloyd Mathew.

The British, who ruled on nominal behalf of the sultans, disbanded the stone-towns' local governments and appointed councils that they thought might be more democratic, based on ethnic differences. These councils consisted of some Swahili patricians, a

Sheikh Athman Basheikh, to whom this book is dedicated, a very dear friend and oldest patrician of the senior subclan in Lamu. He was formerly a *mudir*, or local administrative officer under the British, and a greatly respected elder. He died in Mombasa in 1992. (*Michelle Gilbert*)

few Arabs, an Indian, and a European, always under the chairman-
ship of the local European district commissioner. Since the political
independence of Kenya and Tanzania, much the same system has
been followed, with merely the substitution of an African commissioner for a British one and the inclusion of representatives of the
national ruling party in each country. One can only wonder
whether this form of government is more "democratic" than that
of the centuries-old indigenous councils.

People and Their Families

All Swahili are members of these various territorial and
descent groups, and also of what we may call families. A family is
a loosely defined cluster of close kin, related both by descent and
by cousin marriage. Family members do not necessarily live in the
same house or compound but are usually members of the same
small descent group, tumbo or mlango. One rarely changes his or
her affiliation to a particular descent group, but anyone can change
their family at any time. When married, a man and woman estab-
lish a new marital family while retaining membership of their two
natal families and so linking the two.

Descent forms the basis of kinship clusters formed around
any person. Kin stretch out across the entire society, and often
beyond, due to patterns of marriage. For the closer kin, those in
regular contact, Swahili use particular kinship terms. These are
extended to more distant kin when necessary and may be used to
express common interests or affection: for example, the word
ndugu, "brother," is used widely for friends as well as physical
brothers; or *baba*, "father," is used not only for one's physical beget-
ter but also as a term of respect for any senior man. The use of kinship terms is tempered by rank: a slave might call his owner baba
but an owner would call a slave so only in cases of long-standing
service, trust, or affection.

The household, known as nyumba like the actual building
that contains it, lives together and shares in everyday obligations.
It is the basic residential unit in both stone- and country-towns. It
includes kin and "family," but also husbands, wives, widows, and
widowers, who may come from different descent groups. Almost
all Swahili people marry cousins, some of whom come from the
same small descent group and certainly from the same clan, which
is an endogamous unit. The household may also include various

nonkin, such as domestic slaves who lived and worked within their owners' houses.

An important Swahili institution is the *jamaa* (plural *majamaa*). This is usually translated into English as "family." But the word has an extended meaning. It is a kind of quasi-family, a nonresidential cluster of people who are typically not related by kinship or affinity. It is centered on a particular person, whom they support and help. It is not permanent and indeed may be very short-lived. It is not given a name. It is never a corporate group and can change its composition from one occasion to another. It is an *ego*-centered cluster formed by a patron, typically a senior man who may be referred to as *mtajiri*, "wealthy person." It may include both kin and nonkin who are friends, neighbors, or business partners. We might call them "clients," although the English word implies a more formal relationship than may be found among the members of a jamaa. They offer help usually in money or labor, and at times in political or partisan support, but are never considered as employees or paid in money. In return the patron supports them when they ask him. A jamaa, then, is a network around a central figure, is informal and fluid, and can change membership at any time. The institution makes the formal structure of descent groups pliant and workable in everyday situations, and so is especially valuable in this rigidly stratified society.

Gender

The roles of Swahili men are many and for the most part are clearly defined. There are great differences in men's roles, but in all of them people take great care to appoint men of ability and if possible experience rather than merely following rigid rules of succession. The headship of a lineage by no means always goes to the senior son by birth: it goes to the son who shows the most intellectual capabilities, and it is commonly said that the most stupid son goes to work in a mosque or a lesser government position. It is obviously important to ensure mercantile or financial success in which individual competence counts more than strict rules of primogeniture.

There is greater ambiguity in the roles and lives of Swahili women, which vary from one community to another. Both women and men are subject to the precepts of Islamic law, the Shari'a, but these are followed and interpreted in different ways according to the knowledge and rulings of local judges and religious leaders. Women's formal subjection to male authority is generally accepted, although today with many reservations. Women hold clearly defined rights in property ownership and inheritance—even though a sister inherits only half that going to a brother—and these are rarely questioned.

Variations in women's positions are particularly marked among patricians. Patrician women possessed the quality of *usafi*, "purity," which ensures that honor and reputation, *heshima*, will then be held by their husbands. Patrician women can be powerful people, especially when educated in Islamic knowledge, law, and poetry, and there are few patrician daughters who are not carefully educated in these matters. They control the domestic life of their large houses. It is fashionable, and often justified, to see this as only a second-best role; but for Swahili it is a centrally important one. Wives possess the right of residence in their houses, and their husbands do not. Rights of ownership are vested in the lineage, and female members share in the power of usage and disposal equally with males—although not independently of them. Perhaps the greatest weakness in women's roles is that they are disadvantaged in law: a man's word is traditionally accepted as evidence whereas a woman needs witnesses, although the distinction is not always strictly observed in modern law courts.

The position of nonpatrician women is rather different. They play a far greater part in production, either as wives in country-towns or as women in poverty and without male support in the larger towns. The former are usually the effective leaders of households engaged in food production, so that married women—virtually all women are married at some stage of their lives, and usually more than once—are the stable members of households. Others in this category may be divorced (the divorced rate is high among country-town dwellers), and the women remain in the home to bring up children and to organize agricultural and fishing production. (Husbands who are divorced tend to move elsewhere and may remain absent for long periods.) The women in the latter category live insecure lives in the larger towns; this category is composed largely of women of slave ancestry, whose position was changed radically at the beginning of the twentieth century and who never inherited ownership of land or other property.

Further Reading

Many of the books listed previously also contain material on descent, kinship, gender, and government. See especially:

Patricia Caplan. 1975. *Choice and Constraint in a Swahili Community.* London: Oxford University Press. [An account of Mafia island.]

Patricia Caplan. 1997. *African Voices, African Lives: Personal Narratives from a Swahili Village.* London: Routledge. [Also on Mafia island.]

S. Mirza and M. Strobel. 1989. *Three Swahili Women.* Bloomington: Indiana University Press. [Based mainly on Mombasa.]

Margaret Strobel. 1979. *Muslim Women in Mombasa, 1890–1975.* New Haven: Yale University Press. [A detailed study of Mombasa women.]

Marc Swartz. 1991. *The Way the World Is.* Berkeley: University of California Press. [A close study of family life in Mombasa.]

8

PRODUCTION AND LABOR

The stone-towns were involved as ports of trade in the long-distance African-Asian trade routes until the early twentieth century, and the Swahili pattern of production has largely been determined by that role. Throughout Swahili society and its history runs the paradox that the merchants were dependent upon their distant trading partners and so were in a sense inferior to them; yet as a patrician elite they had to maintain their position at the pinnacle of Swahili society. Much the same situation is found today except that the elite lack most of their former wealth and power, and their position on the East African coast has largely been taken over by non-Swahili immigrant commercial and political entrepreneurs.

Food and Consumer Goods

The stone-towns have never been self-sufficient. When their patricians were rich and powerful merchants they easily obtained food and services from other places along the coast; as a last resort they always had plantation slaves who could grow food for them, although the slaves were used mainly to grow sorghum and other grains (but not the Swahili staple, rice) for export to Arabia. When

71

slavery was abolished and they lost their mercantile position to the Arab traders of Zanzibar, the patricians had no local labor, except that which they had to pay for, and no trading profits with which to do so. Since the independence of Kenya and Tanzania in the 1960s they have seen much of their land taken from them and transferred to more politically powerful immigrants from the over-crowded interior.

The Swahili towns along the coast grow many food crops, but the preferred staple, rice, can be grown in only a few places, and not all by Swahili themselves. Rice is grown only along the banks of the Tana River (by Pokomo people, not by Swahili) and in the few rice plains of Zanzibar and Pemba islands. Most rice is today imported from India and Burma. All Swahili towns produce marine foodstuffs from the lagoons within the reefs, the open sea beyond the reefs, and the rivers and creeks along the coastline. Every town includes shopkeepers who process and sell such things as bread, salt, cooking oils, and other requirements; and there is always at least one food market for fish, meat, fruit, and other per-ishable products. In addition, many new foods are imported from the outside world.

The other area of production has been, and remains, that of artisan construction—of houses, ships, domestic and commercial craft goods, leather, clothing, and other things. The large stone-town houses were built largely by slave labor, which means that it is today virtually impossible to build others. Ships and canoes were and are still built by nonpatrician Swahili labor, much of it in towns known for the particular skills required. The crafts of ship- and house-build-ing, of carpentry and woodcarving, and of leatherwork are all highly regarded and carefully kept in particular families. Sunni Muslim men are not permitted by their faith to touch gold: gold-smiths are either Hindu Indians or descendants of slaves. Behind food and craft production is an immense number of ships, using sails or modern engines, that ply up and down the named stretches of coastline to carry goods between producers and consumers.

No Swahili town is ever self-sufficient: it cannot produce all the things it needs. Its inhabitants may grow part of their basic foodstuffs but they still need other foods, clothing, iron and wooden tools, spices and fragrances, books, paper, and myriad other things. Each stone-town, in particular, is the center of a coop-erative network of producers and consumers These include both Swahili and non-Swahili neighbors, although most networks are formed and controlled by the stone-town merchants and ship owners. Many of these links with the interior date back to the days of slave and ivory trading. Others are modern and with international import-export companies that deal in imports such as films, videos, European cosmetics, and women's dresses. These modern supply networks are almost all outside Swahili control, and they rely as much on the tourist trade as on local Swahili family consumers. Each Swahili network is centered on a particular town, and together they form a complex web of communication and exchange that links all the towns and islands. Its parts are also linked by ties of clanship, kinship, and marriage that together form Swahili "society."

Labor and Slavery

Production requires labor as well as agricultural, marine, and transport organization. As mentioned previously, until the end of the nineteenth century, the stone-towns were occupied mainly by patricians and their slaves, and in the country-towns lived nonpatricians who saw no good reason to go to the stone-towns to work there as laborers. The patricians obtained slaves from the interior in exchange for textiles, beads, and other commodities that they imported from Asia. Some slaves were exported as chattel, mainly to Arabia, whose largely irrigation economy depended upon this forced labor. Others were used domestically in patrician households as laborers, retainers, and guards. The remainder were used as field slaves on patrician-owned plantations to grow food in part for themselves and for the plantation owners, but mainly for export to Arabia where grains were difficult to grow. Some slaves were used for cutting mangrove wood, also mainly for export to Arabia, where wood for building was scarce.

The pattern in the country-towns was very different. Nonpatrician Swahili families provided their own labor for food production, and did not own or use slaves. There were some exceptions— a few Bajun held slaves—but in general slaves themselves consumed much of the food they could grow and were largely uneconomical except as growers of valuable plantation crops for export, as semi-autonomous artisans, or as servants in their owners' houses. When slavery was abolished at the insistence of the British in 1897 in Zanzibar and in what was then known as Tanganyika, and in 1907 in Kenya, the immediate consequence was the virtual collapse of the patrician economy, but it had little direct effect on the country-towns.

Uses and Roles of Slaves

The word "slave" covers several categories of servile people. They were captured in the African interior by local kings and war leaders, brought to the coast, and there purchased by Swahili and later, in the nineteenth century, by Arab traders of Zanzibar. Both Swahili and Arabs were deeply involved in this inhumane trade, a fact not forgotten in East Africa. Some slaves were bought and sold by French traders and shipped to the islands of Reunion and Mauritius; others were purchased by Portuguese traders for export to Brazil.

Swahili people distinguish various categories of slaves: those shipped overseas, those kept as field hands, those kept as domestic servants, and those used as craftsmen and as workers in other semifree categories. The slaves shipped to Arabia and elsewhere were considered chattels: they were not held to be full human beings, and no real attempts were made by Swahili merchants to convert them to Islam. The slaves in other categories were converted, at least to a minimal degree so as not to be polluting to their owners. They were given new names and so were reborn when they entered a Swahili town. A slave destined for fieldwork was known as *mtwana* (plural *watwana*), a word also used for a worthless person. Watwana were owned by particular patrician lineages, worked on the lineage plantations, could be hired out to other landowners, grew their own food, and seem in general not to have been treated harshly. In Swahili society an owner who abused his slaves was despised as someone who disobeyed the Koran and under the Zanzibar sultanate might even have his slaves taken from him and transferred to the sultan's own body of slave laborers. The most serious cases of cruelty appears to have been by Omani Arab owners, who in general despised all Africans.

The other main category, that of slaves for domestic use, was known as *mtumwa* (plural *watumwa*), "one who is sent." Watumwa were closer to their owners and were trusted with domestic and more personal tasks. Male domestic slaves had to undergo circumcision to make them clean enough to work in the owner's houses. Female slaves (also called *wajikazi*, "female newcomers") acted as household servants, cooks, cleaners, and nursemaids. Some trusted

The East African Slave Trade

Slave trading was an important economic activity from the beginnings of Swahili society until the end of the nineteenth century. Slaves were taken to various parts of the coast: some remained as slaves on the coast itself, and others were shipped across the Indian Ocean to Arabia, India, the Red Sea, Madagascar and the Mascarene islands, and in smaller numbers to Brazil and the Caribbean.

The earliest trade was almost certainly in slaves from Ethiopia, and later from throughout the East and Central African interior. For many centuries the main export port was Kilwa, in the southern coast. The height of the trade was in the eighteenth and nineteenth centuries, through Zanzibar, where it was controlled mainly by Omani Arab and Indian merchants; in the far south most traders were Portuguese. The numbers of locally held slaves kept on the coast increased, especially in Zanzibar and Pemba, with the growing of cloves for export, until they were at least 75 percent of the population in the clove-growing areas.

There is continual discussion over the numbers of slaves involved. The most likely estimate seems to be somewhere between ten and twenty thousand slaves a year shipped during the nineteenth century—probably a far higher figure than in earlier periods. This figure would amount to several million over the centuries, equivalent to the large-scale destruction of many African groups in the interior.

female slaves were known as *masomo* (singular *somo*) and were appointed to be responsible for the growth and behavior of patrician daughters, including instruction in sexual matters; they often stayed on as a nurse-companion to the same daughter after her marriage. Slave women were allowed to spend the night within the house, whereas male slaves had to sleep outside. If shown to be trustworthy, a slave might be allowed to work for himself or herself outside the house, as an artisan, crew member of a sailing ship, general skilled laborer, or prostitute. Part of his or her earnings was kept by the slave and part was handed to the owner.

Though not of their owners' lineages, there was often a close personal bond between slave and owner. One duty of male slaves was to accompany their male owners in the streets, dressed in formal clothing with turban and sword and so to act as an aspect of the owner's public personality; on ordinary occasions, however, male slaves wore only black loincloths, without sandals. A female slave might walk in the streets in daytime wearing her mistress' clothing and jewelry. These slaves were known as *wapambe*, "adorned ones," trusted by their owners to be representations or extensions of their mistresses' person, elegance, and wealth. In the past a free woman would not walk outside her house except in the evening, and then only heavily veiled and accompanied by male slaves to protect her.

A separate category of female slaves was that of concubine, *suria* (plural *masuria*). The prefix *ma-* denotes a defined status of some standing (the plural prefix for other slaves was merely the general one for human beings, *wa-*). She would be given her own small house at the edge of the town, was expected to dress and behave elegantly, and was far from the "slave girl" of popular Western imagination. If she bore children to her owner, she would normally be freed and her children counted as the owner's legitimate children. Since her children would be free members of the owner's lineage, her status was of concern for its members and her appointment as concubine would be discussed and agreed to by all the lineage members. She was expected to be freed at or before her owner's death.

Ex-slaves and Their Descendants

The abolition of slavery at the turn of the century affected the entire system of production of the stone-towns and radically changed the positions of both patricians and slaves. Patricians were deprived of their formerly unpaid labor and found it difficult to maintain their high standard of living. The position of the country-towns, few of which had slaves, was not greatly affected; they continued to feed both themselves and the inhabitants of those stone-towns to which they were linked, as they had always done.

Slaves were given their legal freedom but rarely given land. Some moved to empty lands and cleared them to grow grain, which they sent to Arabia as before. Among freed slaves were many women who became leaders of small communities of ex-slaves who had moved to vacant land behind the coast and there grew sorghums, sesame, cassava, and other crops. A few ex-slaves established new and independent towns, the best-known being Witu on the mainland opposite Lamu. Nevertheless, only a few slaves seem to have adjusted in these ways.

Almost all slaves had been deprived of education, had little or no money or valuable possessions, and possessed no land or other property. Many had been made Muslims and so were not ostracized as "barbarians" but had to accept the unwelcome identity of ex-slave. At first, many remained where they were, in their former owners' houses, or became squatters on their former owners' plantations. Those in the former category worked as domestic servants, nurse-maids, cooks, seamstresses, laborers, and in other semi-domestic roles, often as though they were quasi-refugees. I have been told by very old patricians that former slaves were rarely thrown out but instead were kept on as family dependents. This ambiguous situation lasted only a few years and only rarely into the following generation.

The men among them were often able to move away as inde-pendent craftsmen, petty retailers, and laborers. The large towns such as Mombasa were becoming industrialized and had an insa-tiable demand for labor of all kinds. The male ex-slaves knew the lifestyles of the patricians and could adapt themselves as suppliers of general goods and services, as only men were craftsmen and shopkeepers. Most women lived in poverty, whether in houses of their former owners as unpaid servants, as occasional market women, or as jobless women in poorer areas of the towns. The most obvious course was to move into the growing cities such as Mombasa and Dar es Salaam. There women could find work as servants, seamstresses, and prostitutes (an occupation without dis-approval unless too blatant). Their lives, and those of their daugh-ters and sons, were rarely of comfort, but rather of poverty, sickness, and scorn by Arabs, Indians, and others of the new elites of the twentieth century. One response to their generally wretched situation was to join spirit associations, thereby gaining a new identity in the modern world (see chapter 13). Men of slave ances-try gave themselves a rather similar sense of security, identity, and equality to those socially above and wealthier than themselves, by joining forms of religious, musical, or political associations. The men's and women's associations mark a general change from a society based on descent and rank to one based rather on class.

Free Labor

These spirit, religious, and dance associations have affected everyday life, especially in larger towns. But they do not greatly affect the organization of urban and industrial labor except in the field of unskilled work by men and women of slave ancestry. By the end of the twentieth century such men and women were declining in numbers and now have largely merged into wider categories of laborers. They may consider themselves of higher status than the increasingly numerous immigrant laborers from the African interior: they are Muslims and their history is linked to the merchants who had formerly owned them. They are *watu wa pwani*, "people of the coast," and so distinct from and holding themselves superior to the others, to whom they typically refer as *WaAfrika tu*, "Just Africans."

The country-towns still provide their own family labor, and the stone-towns still do some trade with Somalia, Yemen, Oman, Madagascar, and up and down the coast. The larger and industrialized places depend mainly on immigrant labor from the interior, but most plantations depend on "squatters," who are resident laborers, some of slave descent and others being long-resident immigrants, mostly Makonde, Makua, and Nyamwezi people from Tanzania and Mozambique. Squatters are given plots of land for their own use in return for the care and harvesting of cloves and other trees. In the cities, most of the large numbers of unskilled laborers required for work on docks, on railways, and in factories come from the interior as migrants; some are long-term residents and others are on short-term contracts. They are recruited by local patrons who help them as their clients and who make profits both as suppliers of labor to employers and as work-finders for the immigrants themselves. These immigrants, although of crucial importance to the coastal economy, stand apart from Swahili: only a few bodies of laborers include both Swahili and immigrants. Thus in the Zanzibar revolution of 1964 the revolutionary leaders were immigrants who emphasized their "pure" African origins and derided Swahili as non-Africans from Arabia and Persia.

Further Reading

References to fishing and agricultural production have been given in earlier chapters. There are three excellent and detailed studies of Swahili production by servile labor:

Frederick Cooper. 1977. *Plantation Slavery on the East Coast of Africa*. New Haven: Yale University Press.

Frederick Cooper. 1980. *From Slaves to Squatters: Plantation Labor and Agriculture in Zanzibar and Coastal Kenya, 1890–1925*. New Haven: Yale University Press.

Frederick Cooper. 1987. *On the African Waterfront: Urban Disorder and the Transformation of Work in Colonial Mombasa*. New Haven: Yale University Press.

9

MERCHANTS

The Swahili role of merchant between distant and "foreign" traders has been central to Swahili culture, even though only the patrician minority were engaged in the actual exchange. The merchant brokers who controlled this trade lived in the stone-towns, mediating between traders of many cultures, languages, and expectations in both Asian countries and the African interior. These distant traders rarely, if ever, came into direct contact but dealt indirectly with one another through the Swahili merchants of the coast. Over many centuries these merchants came to carry out the specific functions of international cultural brokers: although the majority of the people were fishermen, farmers, artisans, and laborers, the particular flavor of their civilization was determined by the elite patrician role that was expressed largely in terms of occupation, religious faith, architecture, poetry, music, and specifically "Swahili" forms of courtesy and gentility. To comprehend this civilization as it is today it is necessary to look back at this past, as do the people themselves.

The Organization of Trade Exchange

Swahili patricians were brokers at the interface between the capitalist and protocapitalist societies of Europe and Asia on the one hand, and the precapitalist and marginally capitalist ones of Africa on the other. The commodities that were exported from Africa were processed (in the case of human beings, "domesticated") just enough for them to be weighed, counted, and packed for transport by Swahili merchants. The commodities that were imported into Africa were manufactured or processed to a far greater degree. Exceptions to this pattern existed—Arabia exported coffee, and both sides traded in dried fish, tobacco, spices, and other food-stuffs—but the basic pattern was consistent over the centuries and has endured, to include colonial and neo-colonial exchange. On the whole Africa lost more than it ever gained. As noted in chapter 4, Africa supplied natural commodities, ivory, gold, slaves, timber, grains, and wax in exchange for cloth, beads, porcelain, arms, and gunpowder. Today the pattern continues with the exchange of timber, grains, and the natural beauty of their country, for consumer goods from India, Japan, Europe, and America and for money from tourists. The role of Swahili in this exchange lasted until only recently, when they were ousted by big international companies and by the government corporations and agencies of Kenya and Tanza-

---

Trade Goods

The goods traded between Africa and Asia over many centuries are numerous. Those from Africa are almost all natural or raw, merely packed for shipment. Those from Asia are typically manufactured. Apart from Swahili merchants' commission, most of the profit goes to the Asian traders.

The things exported from Africa have included ivory (elephant and hippopotamus), slaves, grains, mangrove timber, copper, rock crystal, copra and coconut oil, cloves, copal, orchella, incense and other resins, rhinoceros horn, turtleshell, hides and skins, wax ambergris, palm leaves for roofing, cowrie shells, sisal, rubber, and sugar. From Asia have been imported textiles, beads, porcelain, rice, gold, silver, brass, spices (pepper, cinnamon, nutmeg), metal wire, arms and ammunition, paper, ink, coffee and tea, wine, dried fish, sacred and other books, films, videos, kohl and other cosmetics, and fragrances such as sandalwood and aloe.

nia. All these can find far greater supplies of capital from the International Monetary Fund and overseas banks than can small merchants of the Swahili kind, however efficient and socially more valuable in the "development" to which the international agencies pay such lip service.

The Swahili trading towns are ports of trade, and they have provided certain uniquely valuable services. Most of the Indian Ocean trade was between very distant partners, of different languages, cultures, and forms of entrepreneurial organization. They used many kinds of sailing vessels, some made in the Swahili ports (as they still are) but most from the Persian Gulf and India. Many had African crews (often slaves) but most ships' captains were Arabs working on behalf of Arab and Indian owners. A trading port had to provide a harbor safe from winds, dangerous tides, and the Turkish, Arab, and European pirates who plagued the Indian Ocean until the nineteenth century when the British finally destroyed them. There had to be facilities where a ship could be

An ocean-going *jahazi*, the great dhow, loading at Lamu for a journey to the southern coast of Yemen, in Arabia. Its main cargo is of mangrove poles for house building: they are visible lying in the hold. It will load there for another cargo for any port along the East African coast from Mogadishu in Somalia to Zanzibar in the south. It probably has a crew of an Arab captain and about six to eight sailors, as well as a few passengers. (*Justine Baruch*)

careened and repaired. The town had to be a place where ships' crews could find sweet water, food, recreation, hospitality, places for worship of many creeds, and personal security. There had to be local agents with means of putting together crews, sellers, and buyers, of giving them financial security to make deals, to find forms of credit, to provide safe storage for their goods, and means for enforcing contracts.

There had to be the complicated coordination of the arrival and departure of large numbers of ships on the ocean side, and of the caravans that carried the trade commodities landward. While the sailing ships depended on the ocean monsoons, caravans had to avoid the heights of both the dry and wet seasons of the African interior. They depended on finding shelter, food, and water, as well as protection from marauders, along the caravan routes.

Organizing all this came to a very tall order, and Swahili towns fulfilled it. If a particular town could not, it was soon ruined in favor of a neighboring town that could. There was perennial competition between the Swahili towns up and down the coast and regular movement of merchants between them, despite their necessary cooperation against the rest of the world and especially the rapacious Arab, Indian, and European colonizing powers that were always waiting to take their profitable trade from them.

Merchants and Brokers

Swahili were the go-betweens in this long-distance system of trade. To play this role they had to do several things. One was to build up networks of resources to ensure a regular supply of goods from and to either set of partners; the supplies had to be of correct proportions, prices, and ready when wanted; another was to ensure the peaceful bringing of trade items to the coast and the exchange of commodities to the profit of both themselves and their partners; and they had to keep the trading partners apart so that only they themselves could act as middlemen and make substantial profit.

Each Swahili trading town established its own networks of trading partners. On the African side these included hunters and gatherers (for ivory and forest products), pastoralists (for hides and skins), and in the more distant interior collectors and providers of slaves, ivory, gold, rock crystal, and other items. On the Asian side there was the need to find both traders who wanted things from Africa as well as those who could supply cloth of many kinds and subtle varieties, beads of many kinds and colors, pottery and porcelain, and all kinds of manufactured consumer goods, including luxury items for the enjoyment of the Swahili themselves. Behind these patterns was the exchange of the four "great" spices of cinnamon, nutmeg, mace, and pepper, and goods for an immense number of purposes including house furnishings, clothing, body adornment, warfare, and religion. For Swahili the African side was the more difficult, with a vast range of possible suppliers and consumers. On the Asian side the Swahili were able to deal with brokers in Arabia and India who were, like themselves, Muslims.

The merchants lived in the stone-towns, where they organized and controlled the actual exchanges of commodities between distant trading "partners" who did not meet. They did not carry out this extremely difficult and complex role on their own. They had to make and retain relations of trust and friendship with both African and Asian traders, most of whom lived in other and distant countries. In modern terms Swahili merchants were the chief executives of international business companies.

Modes of Mercantile Exchange

Anthropologists have long studied forms of "primitive" exchange—barter (even the nonexistent but often suggested "silent trade"), exchange between kin, gift exchange, marriage payments, religious offerings, and others. The Swahili pattern or style was unusual, although not unique. It was found in what historians refer to as "the early modern era" of history, before high colonialism and world capitalism had brought the preindustrial world almost to an end. The exchanges were carefully organized by Swahili merchants in their particular style.

Market exchange is everywhere, typically between traders in mutual competition and opposition, but Swahili avoided—or at least minimized—competition and opposition by arranging that exchanges would be made between affinal kin. A visiting Arab trader could be married to a younger daughter of a Swahili merchant, becoming the merchant's son-in-law, a tie of affinity that was heritable; the daughter remained on the Swahili coast in her father's house, with her children, and the husband would stay with her in the guest room when visiting to trade with him. Most merchants seem to have followed this pattern, thereby avoiding open competition between one another for trading partners from overseas.

On the African side the pattern was a little different although the end result was similar. Younger sons of the coastal merchants went inland to contact the suppliers of goods to be sent to the coast and make agreements for the textiles and beads from the coast the African suppliers would want in exchange. They would marry the African suppliers' daughters or take them as concubines; their children would be Swahili, according to the rule of patriliny, and would stay inland with their mothers. Because these offspring were related to each side, they acted as commercial agents and informants. Exchanges with the Africans of the interior would usually be made between them and their Swahili affines. Many, possibly most, caravan leaders (a position of considerable power and prestige) were these same Swahili men who had African mothers, and would be trusted by both sides to be impartial in negotiations. The pattern was thus one of networks of affinity centered on the Swahili towns and extending into both the African interior and Arabia. In addition to establishing affinal ties with traders, Swahili merchants established affinal ties with the captains of ships sailing between Africa and India. These seamen were almost always Arabs who acted as agents for Indian and other traders. Exchanges were negotiated with these affines within the merchants' houses, places of security and privacy that nonfamily members could not enter unless invited. They were places where open disputes and arguments were forbidden, so that negotiations would be made calmly.

A crucial aspect of these negotiations was that of the medium of exchange. Many Swahili kings minted their own coins, in gold, silver, and copper. Ten silver coins or one thousand copper coins were equal to one gold coin; the various coins were equal in value to those issued elsewhere in the Indian Ocean trading world by Egyptian, Arab, Portuguese, and other rulers. The coins seem only rarely to have been used as actual currency; instead they were used as counters or tokens, owned by the merchants and kept in safes in their houses. As counters, they were used during the negotiations to set values on the commodities to be exchanged. The coins usually bore the names and titles of the kings who minted them, and so were a form of royal regalia that gave prestige to the rulers over the towns and stretches of coastline and also guaranteed the security of both merchants and visitors as being under royal protection.

The exchange negotiations appear to have followed a fairly set pattern, certainly in the case with visiting Asian and Arab trading partners. The visitor first offered a gift, for which no value was set and which was not a trade object. The gift was typically a plate or dish of Chinese porcelain, not used for food but placed as an heirloom in the display alcoves set along the back walls of the main rooms of houses, and then never exchanged again; it would not be on public view, as only family members would normally be permitted to enter those rooms. Other plates were set in cement on family and saints' tombs that were located in the town and its cemeteries. They were thus sacralized. (In recent years most have been destroyed by tourists trying to remove them; they have even been used by local youths as targets for guns and stones.) The negotiations followed, inspecting the merchandise and then using the

The back wall of the owner's room, the *ndani*, in a patrician house. It is covered by rows of small niches or alcoves, and is plastered and lime washed for purity. The niches are to display Chinese and other bowls and plates, copies of the Koran, and other treasures and heirlooms. They are seen only by household members and never by the public, and they represent the wealth, power, and reputation of the owning lineage. *(Photo by author)*

coins as counters. The actual goods would later be loaded onto ships or caravan carriers. After an agreement had been reached, the host gave a banquet for his visitor and they visited a local mosque together. This ritualized interaction closely resembled the pattern of weddings, and since both involve building relations with affines this would be expected. These exchanges were not made at impersonal markets (the small local markets dealt mainly in foodstuffs), but by intensely personal dealing in which "market" competition was carefully controlled and limited.

Swahili merchants faced—and still face—a dilemma. In international exchange they were more or less equal in status and power to those with whom they traded, people of different cultures. But in their own towns they were the patricians, the "great ones" who had to acquire and retain their position at the top of local society. They used trade commodities, mainly cloth, to do this. They imported and owned a variety of fabrics (silk, cotton, and wool) in different colors and designs; they could exchange them for valued commodities such as ivory and slaves and also give them as gifts to friends and rivals and thereby show their own superiority. As in the myth of the founding of Kilwa long before, the gift of cloth to the "uncivilized" local ruler transformed him into a king equal to the Swahilis' own merchant-prince. The merchants gave gifts of beautiful and elaborate cloth, which they alone controlled, to others along the coast and in the interior, and so both built up trust and credit and made themselves valuable supporters and allies in both commercial and political terms. By giving some people high-value and high-prestige cloth and other goods they allocated higher or lower rank to them, and thus could manipulate the system of status on both the coast and inland. In short, theirs was no simple impersonal exchange, measured merely by any objective value of the things they dealt in; rather it was a complex system of building wide-scale and long-term relationships between many societies of Asia and Africa, centered on the fragile Swahili towns along this remote coastline.

The Coming of Modern Trade

In the nineteenth century the exchange system changed with the establishment of the sultanate of Zanzibar, its conquest of the Swahili coast, its takeover of Swahili trading networks, and the building of the Zanzibar City slave market, which soon became notorious for its brutal methods of physical inspection and incarceration of slaves as merchandise to be shipped to Arabia. Zanzibari traders went inland as far as the Great Lakes and the Congo to trade directly with suppliers and purchasers there, including the early Belgian colonial traders coming across the Congo from the Atlantic coast. The inland traders included both Zanzibari, such as Tippu Tib, and also African leaders who thereby built up powerful states. The Zanzibaris used Indian currency, issued and used by Arab and Indian representatives of Indian finance houses in Bombay and elsewhere. The localized and highly specialized Swahili exchange networks were ousted in favor of more "modern" capitalist and colonialist patterns based on market valuations at the fringe of world exchange systems. One of the bases of Swahili society was destroyed, and with it came what Swahili people saw as the disastrous abolition of the second, slavery.

The long-distance trade between Africa and Asia came largely to an end in the form that had existed for centuries, with the rise of the Zanzibar sultanate as an economic partner with India and Europe in the late nineteenth century. During the twentieth century it was in turn taken away from Zanzibar by the rising international capitalist companies based in Asia, Europe, and North America. Even so, the small-scale, personal exchange system of Swahili merchants continues, although on a vastly reduced scale. It deals mainly in mangrove timber, some grains, and tobacco between the northern Swahili towns, Somalia, and the Yemen ports of southern Arabia. Negotiations are still made by merchants and visiting traders in the merchants' houses, occasionally by affines, but no longer using local coins as counters. In recent years most exchanges have been by credit and forms of bank transfer. The use of metal coins is still not liked other than at small-scale local food markets and sales to tourists.

There is also a new form of trade exchange made by the Swahili, in which the beauty of their towns and beaches are traded with visiting tourists, mostly from Europe and North America. The trade—as trade it is—is not made directly with the Swahili but indirectly through non-Swahili African and European entrepreneurs who take almost all the profit. They use local Swahili to provide services such as making wooden souvenirs and renting local dhows and canoes. Perhaps it should not be called trade at all, but merely exploitation of the local people by the new businessmen of Kenya and Tanzania, who know little of and care nothing for Swa-

---

Tourism

The Swahili coast has been a well-known destination for European and American tourists since the Second World War. Most tourists who go to the coast (more stay in the interior to see wild animals) stay in the line of Western-owned hotels from Lamu in the north to Zanzibar in the south. Swahili people call them *watalii*, "those who visit to see [new places]," used in a generally derogatory sense for non-African strangers. Most behave courteously towards their Swahili hosts, but many ignore local customs, especially in wearing immodest clothing and drinking alcohol in public. Such tourists are viewed locally as the last representatives of overbearing colonial rule and are resented and despised, although Swahili people are usually too polite to make their feelings obvious. The recent fear of terrorist attacks has brought tourism on the East African coast to a virtual standstill.

---

hili people whose towns and courtesy they misuse so brutally. Certainly most Swahili resent and indeed often despise the tourists, as well as the non-Swahili "beachboys" and prostitutes.

There are important differences between the two types of exchange. "Swahili"-type exchange, which still takes place but on a greatly reduced scale from that of earlier centuries, may be called precapitalist and precolonial, using both terms rather loosely. "Zanzibar"-type exchange is capitalist, colonial, and postcolonial. The former is based upon intimate ties of kinship, friendship, rank, and trust, all of which tend to be destroyed by the use of impersonal money; the latter is consistent with impersonal relations between traders. Much of the difference is based on technological advances—on fast and reliable transport, efficient administrative security, banking facilities, and in more recent years quick communication by mail, telegraph, and computer. The first kind of exchange was and remains closely linked to relatively small-scale and local competition among the merchants for rank and wealth, and to notions of piety, charity, and religious faith. These features are lacking among traders of the second kind, in their place emphasis being placed on "modern" ideas of class, impersonal competition and exploitation, and wide-scale political power and influence.

Further Reading

Trade and exchange are discussed in the books by Middleton and by Horton and Middleton. More detailed accounts include:

Michael N. Pearson. 1998. *Port Cities and Intruders.* Baltimore: Johns Hopkins University Press. [A highly informative work on the Indian Ocean traders and the Swahili.]

K. N. Chaudhuri. 1985. *Trade and Civilization in the Indian Ocean.* Cambridge: Cambridge University Press. [A classic historical account.]

A. M. H. Sheriff. 1987. *Slaves, Spices, and Ivory in Zanzibar.* London: Currey. [A detailed history of the trade of the sultanate of Zanzibar.]

A. M. H. Sheriff and E. Ferguson (eds.). 1991. *Zanzibar under Colonial Ruler.* London: Currey. [Accounts by several authors of colonial Zanzibar, mainly from a Marxist viewpoint.]

C. S. Nicholls. 1971. *The Swahili Coast: Politics, Diplomacy and Trade on the East African Littoral, 1798–1856.* London: Allen and Unwin. [Contains immense detail of the trade between Africa and Asia.]

Philip Curtin. 1984. *Cross-cultural Trade in World History.* Cambridge: Cambridge University Press. [A wide-ranging history of cross-cultural trade throughout the world.]

10

MARRIAGE AND PROPERTY

Every group of Swahili society faces a basic problem: it must ensure its continuity by reproducing its personnel and composition in spite of the fragility and shortness of its members' lives. Some groups are expected to be short lived: a domestic household or a jamaa group are the obvious examples. Others are long lived, such as a town or subclan. Behind the lengths of their lives is the need for orderly succession to positions of skill, labor, ownership of property, and political and familial authority. Most Swahili social groups are continual and some are corporate: but their members live for only a few years and their lives are divided into short life stages from infancy to old age and ancestorhood.

Perpetuation of the Lineage

Swahili practice a series of transformation rites, known by anthropologists as "rites of passage," that symbolically lead individuals through their lives. The most important and elaborate for Swahili are those of marriage and death. The complexity of these rites varies greatly between people of differing rank, wealth, and power, but all levels follow a basic set pattern, that of the patricians, and are linked to the crucial Swahili notion of usafi, purity.

Purity lies in houses, and also in women, daughters, and wives. A house, especially a patrician stone-built house, is a material structure designed to stand as a symbol of the strength, trustworthiness, and perpetual identity of its owning lineage. Even if it does not stand forever it can certainly do so for two or three centuries, and tombs of famous religious leaders may last far longer. The owning lineage can also last for centuries and its memory far longer, but its membership must physically be renewed every few years by the births of its children. In the Swahili case, the all-important children are the first-born females, who carry on the lineage's identity by their possession of purity, by the practice of parallel-cousin marriage, and by uxorilocal residence after marriage.

The situation for nonpatricians is roughly similar except that they own less property and do not live in long-lasting houses. Their social memories of history and their notions of purity are generally less clear than those of the patricians. Yet they also belong to Swahili civilization and observe its beliefs and practices as far as they consider them relevant to their own situations and ambitions. Their patterns of initiation, wedding, and maturation are essentially the same as those of the patricians, but less complex and less costly.

Initiation

A female or male Swahili baby is merely a living human being and only potentially a social being. For it to attain social personality and maturity is a slow process in the hands of others, culminating in initiation, *arusi* or *harusi*. The degrees and process of the transformation from infant to child, then to unmarried adult, to married adult, to parent, to grandparent, to deceased person, and then to ancestor, are, as in all societies, uncertain due to individual idiosyncrasies. Swahili ideas of an adult person vary according to the adult roles of men and women expected in a patrician family or in a nonpatrician family. In the former, men should be educated merchants; the wives should have become adult and pure women and run their households. Virtually all nonpatrician males become fishermen, farmers, and laborers, and their wives are allotted household and child rearing tasks, both difficult and delicate, and exercise domestic authority that is often greater than that of their husbands.

Modern economic and political development have led to changes in the former positions of Swahili women in their life-careers and their marital and religious histories: they may more easily leave their traditional, often stifling, lives and live as modern townswomen. Even so, Swahili families generally wish their daughters to be made into adults according to accepted conventions, expectations, and methods. To do so can be a long, drawn out, and expensive process, which puts great strain on all but wealthy families. The consequence is that the higher status of wealthy lineages is perpetuated down the generations, whereas the majority of people have tended to become impoverished and therefore possibly unable to observe the full ritual processes that should be involved.

Swahili put together what in English are called initiation and wedding. They use the single term arusi for the transformation of a child into a married adult, a process more important and more complex for women than for men. Women are intimately linked to the purity of both their own bodies and the houses that are a representation of the strength and trustworthiness of the male-controlled merchant lineages. Formal male authority is of little effect without the purity of the lineage's wives and daughters, who are of similar descent by the observance of parallel- and cross-cousin marriage. Swahili do not consider male initiation to be of equal importance, although circumcision is essential for men either as a child or at puberty, as is education in the teachings of Islam. Some groups, particularly the Bajun fishermen of the far north, formerly practiced long and complex initiation rites for boys, but these are rarely performed these days and little is known about them. Initiation for boys lacks the component of inner or moral purity that is at the heart of initiation for girls: adult women must possess an inner purity, whereas for adult men the crucial elements are honor and reputation. It is consistent with this difference that initiation, maturation, and marriage of girls for Swahili are of greater importance and involve long and complex rites.

Marriage

There are several kinds of union between men and women, although not all occur in all Swahili towns. Most are called *ndoa*, from the verb *kuoa*, "to marry." The standard and "proper" union is legal Islamic marriage, *ndoa ya rasmi*, which is registered by a Muslim judge, preacher, or teacher in front of Islamic witnesses according to the prescriptions of Islamic law, the *shari'a*. Ndoa ya rasmi includes betrothal, the payment of legal bridewealth and other money, and it legally permits divorce. The other main legal marriage is *ndoa ya siri*, "secret" or clandestine marriage, which is performed without witnesses or bridewealth. The first type of marriage involves both the husband's and the wife's descent groups, as the young people are expected to be either cross-cousins or paternal parallel cousins (maternal parallel cousins cannot marry). The second type does not involve descent groups but the two parties as individuals, and the marriage may be between persons unrelated by kinship. There is also concubinage, widespread especially in the days of slavery, that does not involve a wedding or registration. It is not today a recognized institution.

Swahili have long been held by others to be a sexually permissive society, especially in that male homosexuality is condoned and widespread. This view is commonly held about most marginal societies and may reflect the fears and conventions of those who discuss them rather than any actuality. Swahili towns have long had a reputation for homosexual behavior between visiting sailors and local young men and boys, as is claimed for probably all seaports; it is accepted so long as it is discreet. Likewise, female prostitution is obvious in most towns, especially those involved in the tourist trade. Prostitution is a recognized way for divorced and poor women to make a living, particularly those women of slave ancestry and without heritable property: prostitution is tolerated and rarely condemned.

Functions of Marriage

Legal and full Swahili marriage has several functions. One is as a means of perpetuating descent groups and of defining their social positions within the total society, that is to say their possession of power and authority over other people and of rights in property. The second is to produce legitimate children. The third is to endow wives with moral purity. The fourth is to link descent groups by forging kinship ties and alliances between them.

Ethnographers usually state that such-and-such a people perform marriages so as to emphasize either descent within groups or alliance between them: Swahili people stress both. At the basis of Swahili marriage is concern with rights in property held or to be inherited by the spouses and their children. A wedding is part of a constant process of rearrangement of the distribution of rights in various forms of property owned by the families concerned. No single ndoa ya rasmi wedding can be understood in isolation, but only as part of long-term strategies of families and subclans for commercial enrichment, increase in rank, the making of moral purity, and claims to social position.

The economic roles of the patricians of the stone-towns and those of nonpatricians are distinct in many ways. The patricians need to ensure that they stand apart from others as rigidly exclusive: they marry close kin so as to retain their wealth, property, and commercial rights in their own subclans and lineages. At the same time they need to make and keep ties of mutual support with both other patricians and nonpatricians and so attempt to be inclusive in relations of trust and interdependence. Nonpatrician descent groups have similar concerns: they need to retain their own property and position, yet they especially want to open up rights, particularly to land, by forming wide, inclusive kin networks by carefully planned marriages. These strategies of exclusivity and of inclusivity are played out by marital tactics, patricians emphasizing the former and nonpatricians the latter.

The most widespread function of nonpatrician marriage is the formation and retention of ties of inclusivity: a marriage is performed to make alliances between the lineages and families of the partners. This is the most common strategy in country-town marriages. As mentioned above, marriages between kin (there are few others) are prescribed to be between cross-cousins and between paternal parallel cousins. These unions have as one consequence the transmission of rights in land and other property to the children from both parents, so that children may acquire rights in widely separated plots of residential and farming land.

The situation is more complex in the stone-towns. Patricians, as merchants, must keep their own exclusive rights in property of many kinds and also form and retain alliances of support with kin outside the immediate lineage, which acts as a business corporation. They do so by arranged marriages, the first between paternal parallel cousins (usually members of the same lineage) and the second between cross-cousins (of different although related lineages). Marriages between cousins are of two kinds: those where they are of the same lineage and those where they are not so. Among patricians the former are carried out by elaborate weddings and the latter by far less elaborate ones. Marriages between cousins of the same lineage are virtually always those of first-born daughters; later-born daughters are more usually married to cross-cousins. The former type ensures both the exclusivity of lineages and also the purity of the line of first-born daughters and so the direct patrilineal line itself; the purity of other daughters is of less account.

Marriages are strategies, arranged by the senior women and men of the lineage or lineages concerned. They are announced by a betrothal after careful consideration of the pair, who must be equal in rank and so of the same subclan, as subclans are ranked. In practice, the equality is a way of denying slave, foreign, or undesirable ancestry. Enquiries are also made about the individuals' moral behavior, whether young men drink alcohol or lack respect for their elders, and whether young women are sexually promiscuous. Betrothal is usually made between children, and even made in advance between those as yet unborn. Those betrothed should properly not see each other before being married, although these days they will probably go to school together and so this is something of a dead convention.

Property at Marriage

Some of the unions mentioned above include the transfer of property from one side to the other; others do not. The general pattern is that the greater the transfer of property, the more important to the groups concerned is the marriage relationship and the more elaborate is the associated wedding.

Property in this context is the cement that links the groups concerned, so much so that in the "highest" forms of marriage, that between patrician parallel cousins and where the bride is a first-born daughter, divorce is properly forbidden: the tie and the transfer of property at the wedding should be indissoluble. On the fringes, as it were, there are in any town many unions without previous betrothal; these have few consequences for the descent groups of the individuals marrying. Some of these unions are fully legal as "secret" marriages, in which there is no transfer of property at all.

Payments of money and wealth are made between the groom's and the bride's "sides." The amounts vary according to whether the parties are wealthy or poor, but they are always agreed upon, some being obligatory by Islamic law, others being traditional without fixed amounts.

There is first the bridewealth, *mahari*, which is obligatory as it is laid down in Islamic law. It must be registered with a judge or a mosque official, although actual payment may wait for many years: it is often regarded as an "outside" obligation, like taxes or tithes. The amount is small, in recent years perhaps a thousand shillings in Kenya. It goes from the groom's side to the bride's father and marks the legality of the marriage and of subsequent children.

There are two other transfers from the groom's side. One is the "donation," or gift, in KiSwahili merely *kitu*, "thing." It shows the integrity and financial viability of the groom. He gives it to the bride and her kin through her father, who may use it as he pleases but usually to pay for the wedding and the gifts he makes to his daughter. The donation may be extremely high, especially when the groom has worked in Oman or Saudi Arabia and made good money. It is often regarded by traditionally minded patricians as a sign of the groom's family being nouveaux riches, and I know of cases where it is refused and the marriage called off because the man concerned was neither related nor of equal rank to the woman's subclan. In recent years amounts have been as high as over a hundred thousand shillings, which has meant that young men without overseas employment find it difficult to marry. It is a personal gift, so is not registered; it is usually not returnable at divorce, although this is often open to dispute. The groom also makes several gifts of money or jewels to the bride during the wedding itself. The groom is the supplicant, and the bride's father is the giver of the bride to him. At various stages in the wedding the groom must make personal gifts before the givers will agree for the rite to be continued. The bride's father or guardian makes return gifts, not to the groom but to his own daughter. One, the *hidaya*, is her dowry and for her use absolutely; it usually consists of household goods and jewels.

Finally the bride's father transfers to his daughter the right of residence in either a new house built for her or in part of his own house. This is right of residence only. The house remains the property of the father's lineage (which is also her own). She cannot dispose of it even if widowed or divorced; her husband (who is a cousin, if possible a paternal parallel cousin of the same lineage) will later give right of residence to their daughter in turn. This practice has been taken by some writers as that of matrilineal descent: this is erroneous as right of residence is never transferred by mother to daughter but only from father (as head of the lineage or lineage segment) to the daughter, and full ownership is never transferred to her.

Marital residence varies from one group or rank to another. That for the first-born daughter is uxorilocal; this marriage is also monogamous and divorce is strongly disapproved. Marriages of other patrician daughters is usually virilocal except for those married to distant kin from Arabia; it may be polygynous, and divorce is permitted. Marriages of nonpatricians are usually virilocal, polygynous, and divorce is both permitted and frequent.

It is often said by Swahili that marriage is *shindano*, competition or bidding as in trade exchange. Like exchange, the process is an ambiguous one whose outcome remains uncertain until it is formally finalized by appropriate public recognition and feasting. Mercantile competition runs throughout Swahili culture, and marriages are no exception: the two "sides" compete to define who exercises de facto authority within the marriage and the ties of affinity created by it.

Divorce

Divorce among most Swahili groups is extremely common. Among the Hadimu of Zanzibar in the late 1950s the rate was well over 70 percent, and among patricians at the same period it was some 50 percent or more (except for first-born daughter marriages, in which it was extremely low and formally forbidden).

Divorce, *talaka*, is permitted under Islamic law. The law permits a man to have up to four wives and as many concubines as he can afford. Today the great majority of men have only one wife although many men have "secret" wives; concubines in the proper sense are no longer found, as the status is that of a slave. A man may divorce a wife, whether by proper or secret marriage, in several ways. He may repudiate her, in a public hearing, by telling her so three times, the last of which is irrevocable (he may later remarry her provided that she has herself been remarried in between). Or he tells a judge that he wants a divorce and in theory at least it will be granted, as the word of a man cannot be doubted; today there is much legal disagreement over the procedure. Reasons for divorce include a wife's adultery, sterility, or persistent quarrelling. A wife may obtain a divorce from a judge if her husband refuses to give her satisfactory accommodation and keep, clothing, sexual satisfaction, or if he become diseased, deformed, insane, or beats her cruelly.

Almost all men who are divorced—and most divorces are initiated by men—soon remarry. The situation is more difficult for a divorced woman. She is formally in a condition of ritual seclusion, *edda*, for three months and ten days. She may then remarry, but whether she remarries or not, the former husband has the legal obligation to support his children for only a period laid down by a judge. A divorced woman with several children, and especially a woman of slave ancestry (which usually means that she has no property of her own), is in a difficult position, indeed often a wretched one.

Rites of Death

Unlike weddings, traditional Islamic rites are carefully performed at death following rules laid down in legal and sacred texts. A judge in Lamu told me that although one may be married several times, one is born and dies only once and the rites must therefore be performed correctly. A corpse must be buried on the day of death, if possible, and certainly as quickly as can be arranged.

How this is done varies. Most patricians, if they live in stone houses, use the room known as "the middle of the house" for the washing and preparation of the corpse. Formerly this was done by slave women of the household; today it is virtually always by specialist women who are usually of slave ancestry and also act as midwives. The corpse is then wrapped in white cloth and taken by bier to the proper town cemetery where it is buried, with prayers being said by a mosque official. The elaborateness depends upon the status and wealth of the family concerned. In a town such as Mombasa or Zanzibar City wealthy families use specialist morticians; these funerals are often said to be for public ostentation rather than for piety.

Widows and widowers are expected to observe a period of mourning, also called edda. In addition, people usually observe personal mourning for long periods: I know of many widowers who have regularly visited their former wives' graves for many years, to sit near them and to read the Koran and poems aloud to them.

Further Reading

There is a large body of writing on Islamic law as practiced on the Swahili coast among the various communities living there. The best accounts for nonlegal specialists and that emphasize the position of women are:

Susan F. Hirsch. 1998. *Pronouncing and Persevering: Gender and the Discourses of Disputing in an African Islamic Court*. Chicago: University of Chicago Press.

Marc Swartz. 1991. *The Way the World Is*. Berkeley: University of California Press.

11
PURITY AND HONOR

In all Swahili communities the most important ritual outside the rites performed in the mosques is that of a wedding. Other family rites, of birth, initiation, and death, affect essentially only those individually and closely involved. Weddings are of wider concern to the descent group, the family, the jamaa, and the whole town. This is particularly so in the case of the "great wedding," *arusi kuu* or *arusi ya rasmi*, that of a first-born patrician daughter.

A Swahili wedding is a rite of great complexity. It transforms socially immature girls and boys into socially complete and adult persons. The transition is made by movements of the persons involved, either moving literally from one place to another or by transferring gifts from one party's "side" to the other. The rite has the framework of a standard rite of passage. There is first a rite of separation, then a period of liminality and seclusion known as the "vigil," *kesha*, and finally a rite of reaggregation. All is movement, spoken words being of little importance, their place taken by dances and songs.

There are many kinds and styles of wedding rites. Every social group, subclan, and even family constructs its own while maintaining that its particular form is the "proper" one. I have been told "there are as many weddings as there are families." Underlying them all is a common basic structure with a single set of aims and functions, expressed by a series of symbolic acts and events. The main variations are between the weddings of patricians, those of nonpatrician Swahili, and those of Omani and Hadrami Arabs. Variations are due to many factors: ethnic category and origin, rank, clan affiliation, occupation, educational standard, wealth, and the personal inclinations of the families concerned. The cost of a large wedding can run into many thousands of shillings, and today only Arab business families are likely to afford a truly spectacular performance. On the other hand, only high-ranking patricians are likely to have enough traditional knowledge to perform a wedding correctly, with the details of symbolic importance performed in their proper order and detail. Most weddings today have ostentation as a main purpose, and this is likely to increase in the future as "tradition" becomes forgotten.

I cannot offer here descriptions of the many types of wedding. It is of more use to discuss one that is in fact rarely performed these days, that of a "great wedding" for a first-born patrician daughter, which may be seen as the prototype. All Swahili people consider these particular weddings to be proper and urbane, and they emulate them as closely as they can. To describe an "average" wedding for all towns and their constituent groups, as has been done by some writers, makes little sense of what actually happens. So I give a description based on two or three patrician weddings of which I was given detailed and seemingly accurate accounts. Men other than the bridegroom and one or two of his brothers may not attend weddings, so I was not an eyewitness.

The Organization of a Wedding

A great Swahili patrician wedding is part of a process that begins with the initiation of the future bride and ends with her transformation into a fully married wife living in a lineage-owned house in which she has inalienable rights of residence. Although she and her husband are usually paternal parallel cousins, the lineage segments associated with each of them are considered distinct and competitive. The competition is played out between them during the course of the wedding until by the end it will have been resolved in favor of the bride's segment, which is seen to have "overcome" the husband's segment: wife-givers claim superiority over wife-takers. The process defines and validates the purity of the bride and her house, a purity that gives honor and reputation to the husband and legitimacy of line to her descendants.

Some people are chosen to play particular roles in a wedding. Each is given specific and complementary tasks. At the center are two senior women, usually called the somo or *kungwi* and the *mpambi* or *mpambaji*. The somo should be a senior kinswoman, usually a maternal grandmother or maternal aunt; in former days she would be a slave woman who had earned the trust of the bride's family and who was given charge of the girl's upbringing. The somo is considered largely responsible for the girl's moral upbringing, and even today many wealthy girls have their *masomo* take them to school and protect them from the attentions of nonpatricians. The mpambi, the "adorner" or "purifier," of whom there are very few today, is also a senior woman of the lineage. She is responsible for the "adornment" of both the bride during her wedding and at all times the house itself: she ensures that the inner rooms are kept plastered and whitewashed and has the formal tasks of looking after the ritual activities that take place in the room called the "middle of the house." She "adorns" so as to make and retain the purity of the house and its women; today her role is often taken at a wedding by a hired practitioner responsible only for the personal adornment of the bride.

Other functionaries include a senior woman of the bride's family known as *mwalishi mke*, the "woman who invites." Her responsibility is to ensure that important female relatives are invited to take part in the wedding activities, thereby defining the effective jamaa of the family. An equivalent but less important duty on the groom's side is performed by the *mwalishi mume*, the "man who invites." There are also women who act as *waandazi*, "servitors," who take care of hospitality. The female kin of both bride and groom sing competitive songs during the wedding. Finally, the close female kin of the bride have various responsibilities in her bodily preparation and adornment, and they help with tasks such as sewing clothes and furniture coverings.

A patrician wedding, the arusi, begins with a daughter's first menstruation. Before her menstruation a girl is a "child," *mtoto*; once she starts menstruating she becomes *mwanamali* or *msichana*, a pubertal but unmarried virgin young woman. She reports the first signs to her grandmother or her somo and is then confined to the "middle of the house," where she wears only drab and simple clothing, eats plain food, is forbidden to use cosmetics or trim her hair. She sleeps on a special bed also used for giving birth and washing corpses. Once she is past her initiatory seclusion, she becomes *mwari*, "initiand."

Prior to her first menstruation, she should already have been betrothed. She should not have been taught about sexual matters until after her first menstruation and only during the preparation for the wedding, which should properly follow immediately. Today this has been changed by the introduction of formal Western education, so that almost all girls are now married after several years in school, during which they should avoid any contact with their betrothed cousins. This is a time of worry for her parents, lest she become involved with other boys, experience sexual intercourse, and even become pregnant. A bride should properly be a virgin at her wedding, although today gossip shows this is not always the case.

The Order of the Wedding

The period of the wedding, which can vary in length, is arranged so that the end of the honeymoon falls on a Friday morning, so that the husband attends the mosque as a fully married man. The entire wedding process involves the invitation of many guests, the preparation of food, and the sewing of clothes, bed linen, and cushions. It may occupy a family for many months.

The arusi is a classic rite of passage that brings about the bride's individual transformation, the bringing together of bride and groom into a single pair, the social construction of a new household, and the potentiality of a new generation. Her rites of separation (which occur at the time of her first menstruation) at the beginning and at the end that of reaggregation (which occurs after her defloration) consist of her lustration, the ritual cleansing by water in the main bathroom. In both cases the washing removes her blood, the sign of impurity, first the menstrual and secondly the hymeneal blood. Each lustration marks a new stage in her transformation.

The wedding proper consists of various phases. After the first lustration is the kesha, the "vigil," the period of *kufuga ukuti*, "to bring out her beauty." This should take three days during which her body is transformed from that of an innocent child to a sexually aware young virgin. The vigil is also the period of activities outside the bride's presence, so that she is "hidden" from them. At

Kufuga Ukuti

This is a key notion in the process of preparing a woman for her wedding. *Kufuga* is a verb meaning to nurture and care for animals, to bring them to maturity by proper care and affection. *Ukuti*, a noun, is here generally translated by English-speaking Swahili as "beauty": it is literally the green shoot at the top of a coconut palm, the shoot that will develop into leaves, flowers, and then a coconut or bunch of nuts. It is surrounded by wood that may be seen as barren in contrast to its own potential fertility. In the case of a bride, this is achieved overtly or physically by preparation of the young girl's body, by its being washed, made soft by unguents and fragrances, and the application of cosmetics, mainly henna and kohl.

A question is whether the "beauty" is given to her by the physical treatment, or whether it is lying as potential within her body and needs only to be brought out by the care and attention of her *mpambaji*. A girl who observes the rules of patrician culture already has the potential for "beauty," best seen in this context as "purity," *usafi*, just as the shoot has the potential to produce a coconut.

the end of the vigil there comes the rite of defloration, followed by the second ritual lustration: when it is said that her blood "replies" to its first appearance. There is then the presentation of the bride as a new wife-to-be, which takes the place of any formal announcement that she is now married. Finally come the seven days of the secluded or private honeymoon, *fungate*, formally beginning with full consummation and ending with a second presentation of the bride as physically and socially a fully married woman. Each phase contains elements that should be performed in a particular sequence, and each contains symbolic acts that gain significance from their place in the entire process. Today, however, only some weddings actually follow the proper sequence, so that much of the symbolism is often lost.

Each stage comprises several acts of both physical action and symbolic meaning. The bride's first lustration marks the end of her initiatory seclusion and she moves from the "middle of the house" to her normal sleeping alcove, where she remains accompanied by only a few close female kin. There is then usually an intercalary day, *siku ya kualika*, "the day of inviting," when the "inviters" issue their invitations (it is an honor to receive one) and make sure that all is made ready for the vigil that follows. During the vigil the bride remains in seclusion while her body is transformed: she is liminal, neither a young girl nor a full bride ready for the defloration by her husband-to-be. Her skin is softened and made into that of an adult with unguents, fragrances, and cosmetics; her hair is cut short, pressed, and straightened, and henna is applied to her hands and feet. Her clothing is merely a *khanga* cloth, an everyday garment that is wrapped around her body. Her body is transformed into that of a fully-grown unmarried woman and her "beauty" is brought out or developed, although not made publicly apparent until after her second, later, lustration.

On the "day of inviting" she is visited by female kin who are received in the courtyard of her father's house (today, often this takes place on the roof) and given tea and sweetmeats. They perform the dances called *msondo* and *kishuri*, both known as *ngoma ya ndani*, "dances of the inner room," inside the house; outside it they dance those known as *vugo*. These all contain sexual references and comment on the progress of the wedding. They are danced only by

Cosmetics and Jewelry

Cosmetics and fragrances are important in Swahili culture. They are used by all women except when working in gardens, and especially at weddings when they are anointed by fragrant oils to soften their skins. Fragrances and oils of incense, sandalwood, aloe wood, rosewater, and many other ingredients are used both for personal adornment and also in rituals to do with spirit possession. Henna is used for skin decoration by brides when their hands, feet, and faces are painted; it is not properly used on other occasions except by prostitutes. Kohl or Western mascara is usually applied to the eyelids. Women also often wear sweet-smelling corsages of bourbon rose petals, jasmine, and basil, all grown in stone-town gardens, worn either on their shoulders or on the hair under the veil.

Swahili women wear gold jewelry as bangles, rings (finger and nose), earrings, and earplugs. Only women wear gold, its use by men being forbidden. Golden jewelry is rarely considered as antique or heirloom, and may be melted down to make new ornaments. Both women and men may wear silver, and women wear precious stones. Gold- and silver-smithing, by Hindu goldsmiths and sometimes by men of slave ancestry, is a highly respected and largely secret craft.

mature women; young women, children, and men are not permitted to be involved, although they may see the vugo as they are performed in the public streets.

On the second or third day the older female kin of the bride go to the groom's house, singing vugo songs. They carry trays of special "soft" and sweetened foods. This is known as *kupeleka mswaki*, "to send the toothbrush." It shows him to be welcome, a potential guest; the "softness" of the food is in contrast to that given him when later he enters the bride's house, when he is given "hard" or "strong" food to prepare him for his defloration of the bride. They are met by a group of his female kin in turn, also danc-

Swahili Dance and Music

There are many traditional forms of Swahili dance and music, the word *ngoma* meaning both "drum" and "dance." They are accompanied by songs. Some are for weddings, others for religious occasions, for meetings of local welfare and spirit associations, and today for public entertainment in halls and clubs and on radio and television. During weddings the female kin of bride and groom sing songs that may be accompanied by buffalo horns *(vugo)*. Some of these are extremely erotic and known as *ngoma ya ndani*, "dances of the inside [of the house]," performed only in the privacy of the bride's house and so not seen by men. The procession of the bridegroom is traditionally accompanied by blowing of the *siwa*, large resonant side-blown horns of brass and ivory. Mosque celebrations of the Prophet's life, known as *maulidi*, are sung by men, often with tambourines. The many secular women's dances include the famous *lelemama* of Mombasa. Men's dance groups, the *beni* (from the English "band") use drums, trumpets, and other European military band instruments.

In recent years the music known as *taarab*, which include sung versions of Swahili poetry, is extremely popular, using both traditional and Western instruments, including electronic ones. *Taarab* orchestras are hired for wealthy weddings, the cost of musicians, star singers, belly dancers, and electric amplification often being the main wedding expense. Other dances today include *dansi*, based on Western dance music, and *kwaya*, "choir," based on Western church music.

The best account is Kelly Askew, 2002, *Performing the Nation: Swahili Music and Cultural Politics in Tanzania*. Chicago: Chicago University Press.

ing and singing vugo in competition. The groom and his male kin eat the food and the bride's party returns to her house. Later that day the groom sends return gifts, part of her trousseau, accompanied by his female kin singing vugo songs.

That same day the groom's male kin perform the *kirumbizi* or "stick" dance. He is seated publicly in an ebony and ivory chair, the *kiti cha ezi*, the "chair of power," used traditionally for a throne or seat of a high official. He should be dressed formally in a turban, an embroidered waistcoat, and wearing an ornate dagger. His kin dance while fighting with sticks. The stick dance may sometimes be repeated just before beginning the honeymoon. It has a complementary meaning to the bride's seclusion: she is the inner member of the new household to be formed by the marriage, whereas he is its potential public representative.

The groom is then taken from the *kirumbizi* to the bride's house. He is welcomed by the bride's senior male kin, her father being absent "for shame," and seated on the specially prepared *kiti cha samadari*, a long chair-like sofa, highly decorated with embroi-

A *kiti cha ezi*, "chair of power" made only by Swahili carpenters of ebony and ivory. They were used by Swahili royalty and by patrician elders when acting as members of a town's *ezi* or government. For a man to be seated on one (only queens may sit on them) is a mark of honor and respect, as with a patrician bridegroom during weddings. *(Nancy Nooter)*

dery. He is invited to ask formally for the bride's agreement to the betrothal and wedding, and when she agrees (she may still refuse at this stage), her female kin anoint him with fragrances and flowers. Meanwhile the two groups of senior women outside together sing *chakacha* songs, which lack the insulting competitiveness of the vugo and emphasize the later joint sexual life of the pair to be married. The groom is no longer merely a betrothed suitor but an accepted future husband. Whereas the bride undergoes her physical transformation in the privacy of her father's house, the groom undergoes no personal physical transformation but a public one from child to fully adult and formally dressed patrician male who is seen as representing the town itself.

The same or the following day the senior men of the two families sign the formal marriage contract and it is witnessed by a Muslim judge or other mosque official. The groom's family gives a feast of coffee and sweetmeats to the kin on both sides and the public, which affirms the legality of the union in both religious and secular terms.

In the evening the bride and groom perform the central rites of the wedding. They begin by the rite called *kumtia nyumbani*, "to put (him) inside the house." The groom, dressed formally in a turban and elaborate robes, is taken in procession to the bride's house, traditionally with the blowing of the town's great side-blown ivory or brass horn, the siwa; this represents the formal participation of the town. Outside the house the female kin of both families meet, sing more chakacha songs, which now celebrate the unity of the two sides rather than emphasizing their opposition.

The groom, with only one or two brothers, enters the house and is seated on the *kiti cha samadari*. He now goes through the rite of *kumtia ndani*, "to put (him) inside." He is first given light food, without rice to show that it is not a proper meal. The somo invites him to enter the bride's room, but at its entrance she bars the way and demands a gift of jewels or money to allow him to enter; this is the "key" to her room. He is perfumed by the somo and seated outside the curtain to the bride's sleeping alcove. He places a jewel in the bride's hand, stretched out through the curtain. Inside she sits on her bed wearing a light shift and veil and unadorned by cosmetics. She is not yet a public person, only a "private" virgin wife-to-be. He enters to sit near and see her, properly the first time they have actually seen each other's faces. They are seated on ordinary household chairs: they are still "ordinary" people with no clearly defined statuses. He blesses her with words from the Koran, and then returns outside the curtain. The somo removes his turban and places it upon the bride's bed and covers his shoulders with the bride's veil and *khanga* cloth. The exchange of clothing symbolizes both their liminal status and their future sharing a single married one.

The groom re-enters the alcove and is given a betel nut by the somo to "give him strength." He is handed milk, which he sips and then offers to the bride, and they are served food without rice (and so not a proper meal). He is given dove's meat, which is considered "hot" and strength giving, while she is given soft and "delicious" food to ensure her passivity. He is taken by the somo to the bride on her bed, and he effects physical penetration without ejaculation. The penetration is to prove her virginity: the somo needs to witness the bloodstained sheet (*kisara wanda*) and show it to the bride's mother and other female kin. It is said that when this is done *arusi imejibu*, "the initiation has been answered or repeated": the first flow of menstrual blood, which she could not control, is contrasted to and "repeated" by the flow of blood at her defloration, a determined act after her deliberate retention of virginity until this occasion.

The bride is taken to the main bathroom where a second formal lustration marks the end of the period of liminality. She is also given a gift by the groom to "thank" her for being a virgin. It is only now that properly the pair may have full intercourse, although many people say this should be postponed until the honeymoon proper: the main point is that she has been demonstrated to have been a virgin.

The following day there is the wedding feast, *lima*, given by the bride's family to her kin. In the evening she and they perform the rite known as *ntazanyao*, "the showing of the soles of the feet." The bride spends this day being adorned with cosmetics, fragrances, and elaborate, beautiful, and expensive clothing. She is then taken to her parents' room, the ndani, and seated on the kiti cha samadari, now moved to the center of the back wall. She is there shown to her female kin who stand in the upper gallery in front of the ndani and look at her through the two doors between. She sits with her eyes closed, in her full "beauty." She is separated from her own individuality by her being seen as though a "masked" woman who has demonstrated her virginity and so her purity. The "mask" is not her "beauty" itself but a sign that it is there, as much an inner as an outer state.

Properly this is repeated on the following days, first to more distant female kin in the upper gallery of the house and later to invited female friends and neighbors in the lower gallery. This is only rarely done today; instead the ntazanyao is usually performed once in a public hall, with dancing, feasting, and much ostentation. Even so, the female kin sit formally, on chairs, without veils (as though at the bride's home), while those of the uninvited public who can manage to crowd into the hall stand at the back wearing their veils. No men may be present and photography is usually forbidden.

There follows the honeymoon, properly of seven days but today rarely of more than three or four; it is known as *fungate*, an archaic KiSwahili word for "seven." At its end the groom enters the congregational mosque on a Friday, to be welcomed as a now fully married Muslim man. Whenever it can be arranged, the new wife undergoes the concluding rite of *kutolezwa nde*, "to be shown outside." She sits, in fine clothing and elegant cosmetics, at the feet of a junior kinswomen who is herself being married and performing her own ntazanyao. After that the bride is publicly recognized as a fully legitimated wife. Today the ntazanyao and kutolezwa nde of a bride may be conflated into a single performance of which the main purpose appears to be public ostentation. An old friend bewailed the extravagance of modern performances of this rite: "We used to make purity and honor; today people merely make money and throw it in the faces of others."

The Wedding as Personal and Social Transformation

I have given a very condensed account of the complex rite known as arusi as it should properly be performed among patricians. It is rarely done today in its entirety, due to the impoverishment of patrician families. In its place are performed rites of varying degrees of approximation to this model, and many observers have assumed that these variants are on the same level as the ideal model. This fails to comprehend the subtlety of the symbols used in the course of the rite, which must be performed fully and in the proper sequence. It should also take place within a patrician house, as the sequence of movements between rooms is a central part of the entire pattern. The whole arusi is a process of conferring purity, usafi, upon the wife and her lineage, of giving the husband the honor and reputation, heshima, that come from the purity of his wife, and of linking the two qualities of the married representatives of the lineage into the single one of uungwana, "gentility."

Further Reading

This account follows the more detailed one in John Middleton's *The World of the Swahili*, which is the fullest yet published.

John Middleton. 1992. *The World of the Swahili: An African Mercantile Civilization*. New Haven: Yale University Press (paperback 1997).

12

RELIGION
AND CUSTOM

A visitor to a Swahili town is struck by the centrality of Islam in everyday life, whether in clothing, the sanctity given to mosques and tombs, the calling to prayer five times a day, the absence of public drunkenness, and perhaps the courtesy and politeness of men and women going about the streets. There are many signs of poverty and of resentment at difficulties and at times injustice, but everyday life is tempered by a sense of order, community, and urbanity.

Swahili people have, and have always had, a set of rites, beliefs, and values that we usually link together as comprising "religion." This is not a book on Islamic theology and I do not attempt to discuss the doctrines, formal practices, and beliefs of Swahili people as aspects of world Islam, but try to understand its place in the social life of the people. Some of what is included in Swahili religion is disavowed by the stricter Muslims of the coast, but this religion should be perceived as a single whole, one variant of the worldwide body of Islamic faith but with its own boundaries and local significances.

The Composition of Swahili Religion

Swahili have been Muslims, of the Sunni Shafe'i school, since the ninth and later centuries as the faith spread slowly along the coast from north to south. We know nothing of any preceding religions that were thereby incorporated or eradicated. In later centuries the Arab colonial rulers of Zanzibar were Muslims of the Ibadhi school, who tolerantly allowed their Swahili subjects their own mosques, religious leaders, teachers, and judges. Ibadhi must be born and not converted, and so they had no interest in changing the beliefs of their subjects. A few Christian missionaries worked on the Swahili coast, but only among ex-slaves and neighboring non-Islamic peoples. They had little impact on the Swahili themselves, even though European missionaries were the first to produce Swahili dictionaries and even the first translation of the Koran from Arabic into KiSwahili.

Many non-Swahili Muslims have often regarded the Swahili form of the faith as unorthodox, even false. However, we should see it as culturally valid in its own right and intimately linked to other aspects of Swahili civilization. We may argue its orthodoxy in the wider world of Islam, the umma, but the Swahili see themselves as also forming their own umma, an Islamic community of its own with the right to select the main points of truth according to their own knowledge of the Divine, their own experiences, and their own practices. So it is fitting to discuss what may, correctly, be called Swahili religion, a particular configuration of rites and beliefs that is unique to them as well as being a part of world Islam in general.

Swahili religion is divided in ordinary conversation into two parts or aspects, known as *dini* and *mila*. Dini is the Swahili word usually translated as "religion" in general, and is defined by the people as orthodox Islamic practice and law as laid down in the Koran and the Hadith. The Koran is the sacred book set down by the Prophet Muhammad on His hearing the words of God; the Hadith comprises the Prophet's comments and elucidations of His life and faith. These writings are interpreted to the living by local mosque leaders and judges who control both the rites of the mosques and the practice of Islamic law, the shari'a. Orthodox religion and law are interwoven, both held as coming from the Prophet's life and teachings in Arabia.

Mila might be translated as "moral custom," and most Swahili people see it as coming from Swahili experience as well as being permitted by Islam. There is continual controversy as to its orthodoxy and propriety. Many devout men and women maintain that much of it is unorthodox as coming from ushenzi, the land of barbarism; some people criticize it as being closely associated with women rather than with men, and even as coming from Satan. It is linked to the acceptance of the many kinds of spirits; although spirits are mentioned in the Prophet's writings, more orthodox people often place beliefs in them as on the very margins of orthodoxy, and in the larger towns today they seem to be fading in importance. Over the past two centuries, during Zanzibar and British colonial rule, Swahili religion as a single phenomenon has become more orthodox, from the traditional and generally unorthodox coastal Islam to being strongly tied to core Islam by Arab reformers and innovators.

Knowledge and Practice

Swahili ritual practice, the observation of religious rules, is based on men's attendance at mosques. Properly they visit the mosque five times a day and invariably on Fridays, *ijumaa*—the name also given to a town's central or congregational mosque. Swahili people also emphasize the celebration of Ramadhan and other annual rites and the learning of the Koran. There are also the five obligations of Islam over and above these everyday rules. The obligations laid upon true Muslims are known as the Five Pillars of Islam. They are the profession of faith, to be made once in perfect form in a lifetime; prayer, properly five times a day; the giving of taxes and charity to the faithful; fasting, especially during the month of Ramadhan; and pilgrimage to Mecca at least once in a lifetime. Not all Swahili people are able to undertake all five obligations, but in general people take them extremely seriously and carry them out as much as they can. The degree of personal acceptance and observance of Islamic rules varies immensely: many men attend a mosque only on Fridays, others attend daily, others five times daily, others only now and again. Only men may enter most of the mosques on the Swahili coast; women remain in the outside courtyard or pray in their own houses. All Swahili women should observe the same rules; many are highly educated in religious doctrine, and all receive a degree of formal Islamic education.

At the heart of Swahili religion is the acquisition and possession of knowledge from God, on which to base both formal and informal behavior. Swahili consider that merely to accept God's powers over them is not enough to make them good Muslims. They must also understand the laws laid down by God and have knowledge of His actions as they affect the world and its inhabitants. They maintain that there are two kinds or levels of knowledge, *elimu*. There is first knowledge of the world, *dunia*, which comes by observance of ritual obligations, the understanding of cosmology and astrology, and the use of divination and of medicines. There is also a deeper knowledge acquired from the study of the Koran and other sacred writings as taught and explained by recognized teachers, and occasionally by direct revelation from God. Knowledge of the world comprises all human behavior that is decreed by God, and includes both what elsewhere might be called ritual and secular activity. For example, to build a ship or house successfully is a sign of knowledge of God's creation and control of the world, from knowing kinds of wood and having the skill to carve them, to understanding the forces of the ocean and its tides, winds, and rains, and to knowing something of the place of houses and ships in Swahili history.

Every Swahili town has at least one mosque and various levels of judges and religious leaders. They are members of local elites of reputation and scholarship, lead the prayers and sermons in the mosques, and are given great respect. Some, known as MaSharifu, are direct descendants of the Prophet and are accepted as having the power to give blessings, *baraka*. Many of these scholars are considered to be saints after their deaths; their tombs are built in many places along the coast and become places of pilgrimage that attract people from great distances.

Swahili do not rigidly distinguish what non-Muslims may differentiate as religion and law. This is so particularly with the practices of the dini; those of the mila are less strictly tied to sacred texts, and indeed there is a well-known proverb *mila ya mji ni shari'a*, "the custom of the town is the law."

The Ritual Calendar

The rites that are accepted throughout the Swahili coast as belonging to the dini include many mosque activities, rites of sacrifice and purification, public fasting and feasting, and giving of alms and tithes. All are based upon the two main calendars recognized by Swahili.

What is usually thought of as the "Swahili" calendar is a solar one said to have come from Persia. It contains 365 days divided into thirty-six periods each of ten days plus an additional period of five days. It begins at the New Year, mwaka (literally "year") or Nauruz (from a Persian word). This calendar is essentially tied to maritime activities involving the tides, monsoons, sailing, and fishing. It is also linked to the performance of traditional New Year rites. Some of these include representations of historical or mythical immigrants landing from the sea; some towns practice the New Year rite of "encircling with the bull," in which a bull is taken counterclockwise around the town, then slaughtered and shared by all members of the town—men, women, and (formerly) slaves. In recent years traditional forms of town government have become of little importance and these rites are rarely performed today except as shows put on for tourists.

The other calendar is based on the moon. People say it comes "from Arabia" and is more recent than the solar calendar. It has twelve months, the last of which is the month of Ramadhan. It fits with the calendar generally used throughout world Islam, while the solar calendar is increasingly less used. This change appears to reflect the reforms of traditional Swahili religion over the past century or more.

In both calendars the year begins at the ritual day of *Id-al-Fitr*, which marks the end of Ramadhan and fasting: it is a day of feasting, festival, and giving alms to the poor. Ramadhan is an intercalary month in which normality is as it were reversed: evil spirits, wandering around the towns at other times, are "locked away"; no food is eaten between dawn and sunset; guests should be invited to the later evening meals; and prayers said during the month are held to have greater efficacy than those said in others.

The center of Swahili religion, as with other Islamic societies, is the mosque, particularly the central congregational mosque of a town. A mosque may be a specially designed and splendid building or appear like any other house except that it has windows and its doors are always open. A mosque holds prayers five times a day, each announced by its muezzin. These are occasions for formal prayers but also, especially on Fridays, for *khutba*, sermons leading to discussions and arguments on local and wider matters, both moral and political, at which all men of the town may give their views. Sets of prayers known as maulidi, celebrations of the birth and life of the Prophet Muhammed, are performed throughout the year, but especially during Ramadhan. There are several

Dancers and procession during Id-al-Fitr, the end of the month of Ramadhan, in Lamu town. The mosque with dome (which is bright green) is the famous Msikiti air-Riyadh, "Mosque of the Sacred Meadows," built in 1901 by the famous Hadrami religious reformer known as Habib Swaleh. *(Dominique Malaquais)*

versions of maulidi, and religious leaders vie in using those with greatest appeal to the mosque congregations.

Not all rites are attached to calendars. The most important are those of sacrifice, *sadaka*, and purification from pollution, *kafara*. The former is performed to prevent pollution, sickness, or harm by spirits. It includes offerings of food given to those attending mosques, serving cooked meat at the New Year festivals, and giving alms to the poor and to children. *Kafara* are gifts usually demanded by the "doctors" who cope with spirit possession so as to remove the sickness and pollution that are experienced by those possessed by evil spirits. The usual gifts are of cooked food, which takes into itself the pollution; it is then thrown into the sea or into uncultivated bushland and the sickness is carried away.

Reform and Innovation

Swahili religious practices have changed over time. The establishment of the sultanate of Zanzibar in the eighteenth century was more than the conquest of the coast by a powerful colonial state. It was also marked by the appearance in the region of the Ibadhi school of Islam. Although the sultans were tolerant of the local Shafe'i school, it had become local and in the eyes of wider Islam parochial. Shafe'i prayers contained more praise of ancestral patrician men of learning and often less of the Prophet and His teaching. The late nineteenth century was a time of deep religious change in Swahili stone-towns, led by immigrant Hadrami reformers. This was linked to the abolition of slavery, the impoverishment of the merchant patricians, the power of the Zanzibar sultanate, and a general weakening of traditional rules and expectations of behavior.

Properly speaking, all worshipped in the same mosques, but slaves were generally regarded as marginal Muslims who had only recently been converted. They were given little education and little opportunity to acquire Islamic knowledge. Many slave owners refused to allow slaves to worship in the same mosques as themselves, although domestic slaves might be allowed time to sit outside a mosque on Fridays, to hear what was being said inside.

The reformers held that their work was to change this situation. The most famous was the Hadrami Arab called Seyyid ibn Alwy ibn Abdullah Jamal al-Layl, remembered today as Habib Salah Swaleh, who came from the Comoro Islands about 1880 and set up in the town of Lamu as a medical healer. His knowledge of drugs and healing was accepted as given to him as part of divine knowledge of the "world." He established close links with slaves and ex-slaves, set up an Islamic school, and in 1901 built a vast new mosque, the Msikiti ar-Riyadh, "Mosque of the Sacred Meadows," where new prayers and even dancing and music were introduced. The great mosque is still important in Lamu.

The composition and range of Swahili society changed markedly between the late nineteenth century and the end of the twentieth. The patricians became impoverished and most of their former slaves were landless and without permanent employment. The former slaves and their descendants became increasingly linked with immigrant laborers and other non-Swahili urban and rural dwellers, forming an incipient single working class. Today many or perhaps most men belong to labor associations and trades unions, but a century or more ago most of them joined the religious associations known as *sufi* brotherhoods. Their members perform rites that by dancing, drumming, breath deprivation, and occasional use of drugs lead to dissociation, forms of ecstasy, and direct awareness and knowledge of God. These brotherhoods are found throughout Islamic Africa and beyond. The most common among Swahili are the Qadiriyya and the Shadhiliyya, which range over wide areas and in which Swahili men are merged with Muslim men of other groups throughout eastern Africa, and so lose much of their former narrow ethnically defined identity and authority.

In the past few years there has been another wave of reformers, mainly of the Shi'a school, from Kuwait and Iran. These reformers, Shi'ites, are strongly opposed by most Swahili religious leaders but have gained supporters largely by giving gifts of black silk veils of modern style and air tickets to Mecca to ordinary citizens who attend their religious services. The earlier Hadrami reformers represented the wider Islamic world of the Indian Ocean, and the new Shi'ite reformers analogously represent a new world of "modern" Islam.

Swahili Islam today has been weakened in its authority and importance outside the everyday lives of its adherents. Most government agencies, hospitals, schools, and modern commercial companies are staffed by Christians and distrusted by many Swahili. Younger educated Swahili men and women take employment in Christian undertakings, thus their everyday working lives are in the company of non-Muslims. Religious adherence becomes a wider social and political weapon, and Muslims often try to ensure its acceptance and continuity by supporting forms of religious reform and purification from outside East Africa.

Further Reading

There is no single account of Swahili religion. The best is:

Randall Pouwels. 1987. *Horn and Crescent: Cultural Change and Traditional Islam on the East African Coast, 800–1900*. Cambridge: Cambridge University Press. [A detailed and scholarly history.]

Other useful accounts are:

Susan Hirsch. 1998. *Pronouncing and Persevering*. Chicago: University of Chicago Press. [Emphasizes law over religious practice, but thorough.]

A. H. M. el-Zein. 1974. *The Sacred Meadows*. Evanston, IL: Northwestern University Press. [A detailed study of a Lamu town.]

13

WOMEN, MEN, AND SPIRITS

Swahili religion, like any other, is never static. Both the dini and the mila undergo continual change. The changing beliefs and practices are especially those about spirits and held by nonpatricians, as they have much to do with peoples' responses to poverty. Although many devout Swahili deny the importance of the beliefs and practices to do with spirits, especially when speaking with non-Swahili visitors, they are very much part of Swahili religion.

The Place and Nature of Swahili Spirits

People who have written about religious beliefs and practices in Africa generally hold that the observance of formal Islamic rules is associated more with men than women. Women are more likely to be linked to spirits, and this appears to be generally so for Swahili people. Swahili women do not belong to the sufi brotherhoods, but they do practice rites of dissociation in the form of spirit possession, and they join spirit associations that are found throughout the coast.

Swahili people consider spirits to be in one of two categories of intermediaries between the living and God. As in perhaps all religions, one category comprises those who have lived as human beings—ancestors and saints (once living Islamic scholars with powers of wisdom and blessing)—and the other includes those who have not lived as human beings—angels and spirits. Swahili hold that there are several kinds of spirits, who are specific to Swahili: whereas the dini is considered as essentially the same throughout Islam, the kinds of spirits vary in detail and are often held to be either pre-Islamic or recent intrusions into the local world.

Swahili hold that there are many spirits, each town or area having its own. Each spirit is attributed its own name, location, powers, characteristics, ways of contacting the living, and type of appeasement demanded by it when it possesses a living person. Spirits are generally invisible to the living, although some can become apparent or audible. Swahili say that there is no spirit world apart from that of the living: the spirits live near and in human settlements and may be encountered at any time except during Ramadhan. Encounters with them include both their possession of and their conjuring by living people.

There are two main kinds of spirits in Swahili religion, the *mizimu* (singular *mzimu*), and the *majini* (singular *jini*). The mizimu are generally considered to be spirits who were at one time living and associated with particular places. The majini are not linked to ancestors, and they may be encountered anywhere.

Mizimu are, for the most part, local, living in and near places that they "own." The living give them offerings in the form of

---

Words for Spirits

Spirits are not fully human but are treated very much as though they were. The various categories are given distinct grammatical forms for the plural nouns.

A spirit linked to a particular place, *mzimu*, has the plural *mizimu*: the prefix denotes that it is living but not human, like a tree. *Mzuka*, a specter, takes the plural form *wazuka*, which is used for ordinary living people. *Pepo*, the general word for human-like spirits, takes the neuter plural *pepo*, indicating that it is a general, collective word and is composed of many subtypes of living and human-like possession spirits. These take the plural form *ma-*: *jini* has *majini* for plural; *rohani* and *shetani* take plurals *marohani* and *mashetani* respectively, as virtually living human beings who can have sex with and even marry humans and bear children with them.

incense, *ubani*, which is their "food." They live underneath objects such as rocks or large trees, or in caves, and those who give them offerings place a white flag there. They become dangerous to people who try to open up a piece of land that the spirits consider to be theirs. To avoid and placate them the would-be occupant makes an offering to them through the agency of the settlement's mzale, who is usually a woman. In the same way, a living tenant pays rent to the living owner of a plot of land; this is in the form of money but is also called ubani.

People say that the majini were the first inhabitants of Earth, placed here by God. They lived in Paradise but followed Iblis (Satan) who was thrown out by God because he insisted that he was of higher standing than Adam, the first created human being. Some majini are said to be Muslims and to be good. Others chose to live outside Islam with "barbarians" (including those who could be enslaved). They can all cohabit with and at times even marry living people and bear children with them. The good ones cohabit or marry with those of free ancestry and in the past the evil ones did so with slaves, although that distinction is rarely heard today.

There are several types of majini. The most common are the *pepo* (singular *pepo*), which means "wind," from a root word that means to sway about, as people do when possessed by them. There are many kinds of pepo, all of whom are said to seize or possess people who come near them. Any pepo or other spirit may possess many women, usually those who are kin or neighbors. Other majini include those known as *mizuka* or specters, whose appearance is frightening but usually bring no harm for those who see them, and *shaitani*, "satans," considered to be evil, dangerous, and closely associated with people of slave ancestry. There are many other types of named spirits in various places along the coast; many become popular for a few years and then vanish, their places being taken by new spirits who are considered to be more fashionable—they may like new forms of dress, music, or cosmetics among their adherents.

It has often been suggested that women are possessed more than men because of their social deprivation: to be possessed bonds them together as women seeking equality to men. This argument cannot be upheld for the simple reason that although most women in any society may well consider themselves deprived, not all are possessed. A more likely factor is the ambiguity of the status of so many women in both traditional and modern African societ-

ies. Spirit possession, at least among Swahili, seems to be a fairly
modern phenomenon. It dates perhaps from the later part of the
nineteenth century, when the position of women (especially slave
women) changed radically.

Possession by the Spirits

The term "spirit possession" refers to the seizure or possession of a person's mind and body by a believed spirit: a pepo is
said to "ride" its victims or to use them as chairs or seats. The spirit
is thus superior and controls the person possessed. Possession is
recognized by the victim's shaking movements and bizarre speech,
as the spirit may speak using the victim's voice and body. However, we may see the process rather differently, that it is in fact usually the victim who makes the decision to be possessed, as a
deliberate and conscious act. Possession is part of a culturally
defined process of personal adjustment to living in a difficult social
environment; it is not an isolated happening but part of the long
process of a person's development. A better term than "victim"
might often therefore be "host," and it is problematic whether host
or spirit is actually in control.

A person who is possessed usually consults a specialist
known as *fundi*, a "craftsman," who may exorcize the spirit. This is
done at a special occasion, may take a long time and be expensive,
and can be mentally and physically painful and distressing for the
person concerned. Or the relationship may continue: I have been
told that the actual possession is "like a wedding" and may continue for a long time, like a marriage. To varying degrees of consciousness by the host, possession is often held to be a sexual
relationship, imagined but perhaps nonetheless real in the victim's
experience. Possession by a spirit is not usually considered a form
of rape, although those possessed by a shaitani may claim so.

Usually a possessed woman joins an association of people
(almost all of whom are women, although men are also possessed),
controlled by a specialist known as *mganga* or *mwalimu*. The first
term means "doctor" with particular reference to "African" skills;
the second means "teacher," which emphasizes his or her being a
knowledgeable Muslim. The word for such an association is *chama*,
a word used also for a coven of witches, a modern political party, a
caravan from the interior, a military unit, and for other common
interest and mutual support groups of people unrelated by kin-

ship. There are many such associations among Swahili women, some formally linked to Islam, others to spirit possession. The associates meet to dance, sing, recite poems, go sea bathing or on picnics, and to contact their possessing spirit who may help them in their everyday lives, as would a living husband. Other associations are purely secular such as the famous lelemama associations of Mombasa.

"Doctors" and "teachers" are professionals who are thought—and paid—to control the activities of spirits and may be given much respect and prestige. They help those who are possessed and in psychological distress to adjust to a world that can be cruel and unjust in light of their memories of the past and hopes for the future. Spirit possession is often held by writers to be a particular and perhaps exotic religious phenomenon; but it should also be considered to be normal and expected in a modern society in which differences between rich and poor become increasingly marked and harmful. Most women who claim to be possessed and then decide to join a chama association tend to be poor, divorced or widowed, and frequently physically ill. These conditions are anomalous. Some women are poor in what was in traditional memory a wealthy society and where today there is obvious evidence of "new" wealth that does not reach them. Others have continual ill health, especially gynecological problems, in a society where women are expected to marry, become respected wives, and bear children. This is an outwardly formal and highly stratified society, of traditional mercantile wealth, but these days the lower half of its people live in impoverishment and with social uncertainty and fear in the modern and, to them, hostile world.

There are many spirits and different categories of women who become their "wives." A weakness of many accounts is the uncritical use of the word "women": we need to ask "which women?" We may divide "Swahili women" into at least three categories that are used by the women themselves: patricians; nonpatrician women of free ancestry; and those of reputed slave ancestry, typically the really poor at the bottom of the system.

Patrician women may experience personal fears and disappointments similar to those in the other two categories, yet their proper role is still that of the pure wife of a successful merchant. There are, in some stone-towns, majini known as *marohani*: most are male and become spirit-lovers or -husbands of usually wealthy married women, who may claim to have spirit-children by them.

These women claim deliberately to conjure their spirit-husbands, who come from non-Swahili groups with whom the patricians formerly traded. They include Arabs, Somali, Ethiopians, Indians, Chinese, Europeans, and some neighboring Africans who were often considered more powerful than Swahili themselves. This recalls the mercantile practice of creating ties of affinity with trading partners, but now in the postcolonial world it is the wives who take control. One such woman, highly educated and fully aware of what she was doing, told me that the patricians lost their wealth because of their incompetence: as is too often forgotten these days, all depended upon their wives, and does so still. At the other end of the social scale, many of the women who are really poor, and of slave ancestry, claim to be possessed by shaitani spirits that come from the African interior. This gives them power, a mystical equality with other people, and analogously reminds people of their crucial place in Swahili history, usually ignored in written accounts. The possessed and their "doctors" are writing a reformed history in which a clearer and more deserved place is given to Swahili women whose roles were so seriously weakened under Arab and British colonization. This "new" view of Swahili history is formed and sanctioned by God and made apparent to the living by the spirits, who are God's creatures and add to the knowledge of His designs possessed by His living creatures. As always, ritual removes confusion and untruth to make order and purity.

Powers of Evil

Many devout Swahili Muslims may be uncertain how to regard spirits, but they have little doubt as to the evil of those living people who are thought to practice witchcraft and sorcery. Spirits are usually considered to be morally ambiguous, capable of helping or of harming living people; they are not considered to be human beings even though they may consort with the living. But some living people are held to be harmful to their fellows, willingly and deliberately bringing them misfortune and even death. Knowledge, elimu, is good, but witches and sorcerers pervert it for their own ends. They are fellow-members of society but act as self-willed traitors living safely and secretly within their own towns, wards, and kinship groups.

People generally recognize two types of mystical evildoers: witches and sorcerers. Both English words refer to methods of harming others and not merely to different types of practitioners as such; indeed, many evildoers use both methods. We may doubt the reality behind the beliefs, but it is the beliefs that are significant to understand the phenomenon.

A witch, *mwanga*, is thought to have innate power to harm others or to acquire it from other witches. A sorcerer, *mchawi* or *mlozi*, uses material objects or "medicines" to bring harm to others. Both can be countered by a mganga, "doctor," who can also deal with spirits. Witches are the more feared, and are held usually to be women who may despoil graves and eat corpses. They belong to secret covens, *vyama* (singular, chama, the same word used for spirit associations). Witches are utterly evil, while sorcerers can be purified by possession and treatment. Witches are said to meet at night and to offer their own children, or those of their kin, to their peers to be eaten, a form of meat known as "a cow with two legs." Eating one's own children, the members of one's husband's descent group as well as of one's own, destroys the future of that group. In addition, the mere presence of a witch can be potentially dangerous to a lineage whose success in the competitive mercantile world is due to the purity of its wives and the reputation and honor of its men. Witches can irrevocably destroy the success of their lineage.

These beliefs are consistent with those about possession by spirits, which affect women more than men. In all Swahili towns the roles of women are ambiguous. Among patricians the reputation of men depends upon the purity of their wives and sisters, a spiritual condition brought about by the deliberate action of the women. Among nonpatricians de facto authority within households is exercised mainly by the wives and senior woman, and there arise many situations of gender resentment. Sorcerers are usually thought to be men who harm their enemies by mystical means; they work individually and not in covens, perhaps a reflection of the past practice of competitive merchants. Those women believed to be sorcerers are thought to have slave ancestry or to be of poor households, resentful of the wealth of others related to them but not sharing their good fortune.

Other evildoers are those men and women said to make and control zombies, *'ngi'nginge*, who work for them at night or may be sent, wearing metal claws, to kill others. Both men and women are thought to use drugs, especially datura weed, to make others act as killers. Zombie-masters are usually believed to be Arab landowners who use ordinary men to make them rich. This belief is also held about modern nouveaux riches, whose sudden wealth requires both explanation and reaction. The newly rich may be suspected of being helped by spirits, of using zombies, or of harming their business rivals by sorcery. These are mysterious crafts not unlike the skills of successful artisans, of shopkeepers selling modern consumer goods, including drugs, or even of successful prostitutes working among tourists. The pattern is that of Swahili order and propriety being threatened by cultural traitors with powers derived from non-Muslim and "African" sources, a modern reaction to the troubles brought by the globalization over which ordinary people have no control.

Further Reading

Three excellent sources are:

Patricia Caplan. 1997. *African Voices, African Lives*. London: Routledge.

Michael Lambek. 1993. *Knowledge and Practice in Mayotte: Local Discourses of Islam, Sorcery, and Spirit Possession*. Toronto: University of Toronto Press.

Peter Lienhardt. 1968. *The Medicine Man, Swifa ya Nguvumali, by Hasani bin Ismail*. Oxford: Clarendon Press.

14

SWAHILI VOICES

In the beginning of this short book I wrote that the two usual questions asked about Swahili people are "Who are they?" and "What is Swahili civilization?" To answer them we need to ask who is asking and who is answering. The previous chapters are woven around both the questions of definition and of the identities of those who ask and answer.

Swahili people form a society whose composition and boundaries are redefined from one time period to another. The principal factor causing this fluidity and uncertainty has been the pattern of trade between Africa and Asia in which Swahili patricians have played the central role of middlemen-merchants. The establishment of colonial rule by the sultanate of Zanzibar and the later abolition of slavery by the British were part of this same history. On the African side the Swahili traded with partners throughout the eastern interior, their identities and the goods they produced and consumed varying over history. The same was true on the Asian or Ocean side, with partners including Arabs, Indians, Chinese, and Europeans; the goods they wanted and produced likewise varied over time. Swahili people have inhabited various towns and stretches of the coast, but they should be seen as occupying and controlling the center of a wide field of exchange, rather than forming a strictly bounded and isolated society.

The interplay between "Swahili" and "Zanzibar" has been and remains crucial to understanding the Swahili, even if not to be exaggerated. Many local historians see Zanzibar at its center and the Swahili towns as dependent and marginal; they attempt to "Africanize" the "Arab" component of the coastal population, so as to legitimize the sultanate by transforming it from a colonial power into a colonial dependency and to absolve it from responsibility for much of the African-Asian slave trade. This present book shows the other side, that of Swahili people themselves. This is not to accuse the historians of falsification: the two views of the same society are from the vantage points of these two main elements, but both views are "true."

We can understand Swahili society and its civilization not only by seeing them over space but also over time. As previous chapters show, this is difficult. It is easier to describe and analyze a society and its culture at a single point in time, whether done by an anthropologist for the present or by a historian for the past. What is needed is to do both, to portray this particular society as a long-term process of construction and adjustment of networks of mercantile and social relations and of cultural obligations and expectations. I have tried to do this.

Much has been talked of the notion of *la longue durée*, to perceive the life of a society over a long period. The study of a society over a great length of time is difficult and in many cases impossible due to lack of evidence, whether archival, archaeological, historical, or ethnographic. It is, however, possible to some extent in the case of Swahili, mainly because there are written records. And people's collective memory, both oral and written, is very much a part of their being merchants with so wide an experience of exchange relations with other people.

I have tried to describe and analyze the structure of their society, always changing, usually slowly but on occasions suddenly, as with the abolition of slavery and the 1964 revolution in Zanzibar. There are a few constants: mercantile exchange, forms of corporate local and descent groups, patterns of stratification, and Islam. The internal organization of Swahili society, the pattern of relations between constituent groups or communities, has remained unaltered for very long periods.

The link between occupation and claimed ethnic identity is not rigid, and ethnic affiliations may be associated with different occupations at different times. The pattern found today is not that found in 1500 or in 1850. The principal reason has been the change in world trade patterns, especially those of the Indian Ocean, from about the sixteenth century when the Portuguese took over much of the Arab trading control of the Ocean, until the twentieth century, when the abolition of slavery and the flowering of early capitalism in Zanzibar changed forever the control of the African-Asian trade by Swahili merchants.

Swahili, like most other peoples, see themselves and their civilization in terms of morality: in their own case, ustaarabu, traditional civilization, and utamaduni, urbanity, standing together against an all-surrounding ushenzi, barbarism. In past times this confrontation was against a greedy and cruel sultanate, and today is against what they see as the increasingly unjust difference between rich and poor, a polarity brought about by the outside world and its "development" policies. They themselves hold clear memories of their history and its link to their present decline, impoverishment, and loss of political power. History is seen as morality, the fate of humankind as determined by God, and is known to the collective memory of Swahili people.

Memory has many forms. For Swahili people one of them is interpreting the meanings of the material ruins of past towns that

---

Proverbs

Swahili people give great importance to the use of proverbs in their everyday lives and to use them well is considered to make speech elegant and to avoid being blunt and impolite. Like Swahili poetry, they contain many circumlocutions and subtleties of meaning that are often difficult for others to understand. To understand them well shows the speaker to be a "real MSwahili." Some examples are:

Biashara haigombi. Trade does not quarrel.

Used by shopkeepers when customers argue about the price.

Kilemba hakimfanyi mstaarabu mtu. A turban does not make a man civilized.

Dunia haina mwisho. The world has no end.

Used to tell someone that the world will outlast him.

See Albert Scheven. 1981. *Swahili Proverbs.* Lanham, MD: University Press of America.

are visible throughout the coast. One of the best-known and quoted KiSwahili poem is called *al-Inkishafi*, which has many translations. The most recent is by James de Vere Allen, who translates the title as *Catechism of a Soul*; an earlier translation by William Hichens was titled *The Soul's Awakening*. The poem was written by Sayyid Abdalla bin Ali bin Nasir in about 1820 and deals with the glories and decline of the northern town of Pate, once a place of power and wealth and today merely a small town at the end of a shallow muddy creek.

The central verses of this long poem are

How many wealthy men have we not seen
Who in their splendor shone like the sun itself,
Strong in their great hoards of ivory,
Powerful in stocks of silver and of gold?
To them the whole world bowed down in homage,

For them the Road of Life was broad and straight.
They went their ways in arrogance, unafraid,
Heads high in air, their eyes screwed up in scorn.
They swung their arms and tossed their haughty heads,
Retainers went behind them and before.
Wherever they went they took the seat of honor
And many bodyguards surrounded them.

Their lighted mansions glowed with lamps of brass
And crystal, till night seemed like very day;
And in their halls dwelt Beauty everywhere
And veneration stalked them all their days.
Their homes were set with Chinese porcelain
And every cup and goblet was engraved
While, placed amidst the glittering ornaments,
Great crystal pitchers gleamed all luminous.
The rails from which they hung the rich brocade
Were made—I swear by God, Source of all Wealth—
Of teak and ebony, row upon row of them,
Rank upon rank with fabrics hung displayed.

The men's halls hummed with chatter, while within
The women's quarters laughter echoed loud.
The noise of talk and merriment of slaves
Rang out, and cheerful shouts of workmen rose.

And when they went to rest, they had massage
And fans and gay-robed women for their ease
And music-makers, playing and singing songs
Ceaselessly till they slept. And when they slept
It was on exquisite beds of finest timber
Carefully chosen, with soft mattresses
With pillows of green cloth at head and foot
Embroidered with silver thread and fine-spun gold.
Fabric was draped on canopies above
To shelter them. Their limbs were sprinkled over
With rosewater, and their bodies anointed
With attar and sandalwood and incense-smoke.

And yet, for all their wealth and proud grandeur
They took, with Death's great Caravan, their leave
And journeyed to the mansions of the grave
And crumbled like blowing sand, and came to dust.
So sleep they now, in a city of a finger's span.
No curtains there, no cushions nor silk couch.
Their bodies are broken, mutilated all
And crushed by the merciless constraint of tombs.
Their cheekbones have caved in and decomposed,
And pus and blood ooze through their parted lips;
Maggots infest their nostrils and their throats
And the beauty of their countenances is transformed.

They have become food for insects and for worms,
Termites and ants devour and bore them through.
Their bodies are eroded. Venomous snakes
And scorpions coil in the cavities.

Their lighted mansions echo emptily;
High in the painted rafters flutter bats,
There are no murmurings, no happy shouts,
And on carved bedsteads spiders spin their webs.
Owls hoot in the solitude of the ruined halls
And quail and gamebirds scuttle and cry below.
On painted curtain-rails now vultures perch,
And young doves pout and coo between themselves
Or start, and flap their wings, and whirr away,
Swallows build their nests, and wood-pigeons.

Cockroaches rustle in the empty courts.
Where once men gathered, now the crickets shrill.

The chatter in the anterooms has ceased
And there remains only dirt and foul decay.
Bushes are canopied over with wild vines,
Men fear today to pass these yawning doors
For inside, Silence and Darkness reign supreme.
If you believe me not, and say I lie,
Then go yourself and peer about those halls.
Call out. Your echo will come back, naught else,
For human voices can be heard no more.